The Marriage MIRACLE™

TRUTH: THE SECRET INGREDIENT

Paul Kendall

© 2012 Paul S. Kendall

Dedicated to:
Rundle and Cinda Smith
The counselors who saved our marriage
seventeen years ago.

CONTENTS

Introduction — 5

Chapter One
A Better Understanding of Your Spouse — 9

Chapter Two
Feelings and Communication Skills — 23

Chapter Three
Understanding and Expressing Anger — 35

Chapter Four
Emotional Maturity — 49

Chapter Five
How to Have a Healthy Disagreement — 64

Chapter Six
The Importance of Forgiveness — 74

Chapter Seven
When Selfishness Connects With Authority — 86

Chapter Eight
Breaking the Vicious Argument Cycle
    (Husband's Role as Leader) — 95

Chapter Nine
Wife's Role as Helper   108

Chapter Ten
Emotional Needs   118

Chapter Eleven
Fulfilling Emotional Needs   128

Chapter Twelve
Conclusions   136

About the Author   140

Introduction

Truth, that's what you've opened this book to find; you want information that is solid and trustworthy. You need truth because truth always works, just like two plus two always equals four. Truth will work in your marriage every time, regardless of your circumstances.

"The Marriage Miracle" would be a facetious title for a book if it were based on a man's theory but this book is not based on man's theory; it's based on the most trustworthy source of wisdom—God's Word.

Isaiah 55:11 says that *"God's Word will not return void;"* how is that possible? Because God's Word is truth, and truth always works. That scripture goes on to say that whatever His Word is spoken into will prosper; it prospers because the truth replaces the lie and when your decisions and actions are based on truth your circumstances begin to change. This book is filled with Biblical principles of truth that will bring new life to your marriage if you simply apply them.

As you read these pages, you will learn techniques that when applied to your marriage, will always work. Now I know the idea of learning techniques may sound less than exciting, until you realize that you are already using them in your marriage. The problem is they are not working; you're not getting the results that you desire. Therefore, your greatest challenge in this book will be to replace your ineffective techniques with new ones, based on principles of truth.

Isaiah 43:18-19 says, *"Forget the former things; do not dwell on the past. See, I am doing a new thing! Now it springs up; do you not see it? I am making a way in the wilderness and streams in the wasteland."*

If you are facing extreme challenges, that scripture might be difficult to believe, but God *can* do something new in your marriage.

My wife Evie and I have been married for nearly 30 years now, but in our 13th year of marriage we hit rock bottom. It was a very, very dark time. We were two signatures away from a divorce and basically just trying to decide what would be best for our two children under the circumstances, when somebody suggested that we go to marriage counseling. I didn't like that idea because I always considered myself to be the helper and not the helpee. Besides, I was a minister and truthfully I was pretty embarrassed to go.

But I decided to go for one reason only: so that after my divorce, I could look my two children in the eyes and tell them, *"I tried everything to make it work with your mother... even counseling!"* It was definitely the wrong reason to go, but it got me there. At our first appointment, the counselors told Evie and me that they wanted us to join a twelve-week group program with five other couples. The idea of counseling was bad enough—the thought of being in a group seemed like sheer torture! I resisted, but these counselors wouldn't do it any other way, so we signed up for the next group. On top of the frustration of having to participate in a group, our meeting location was 45 minutes away. The last eight miles was down a washboard-like road and one week I lost my muffler! We even had to get our own child care which was very difficult for us to do because our meetings were on Sunday mornings, but we were determined to try.

We went on to learn things in that program that we had never heard before. At the end of the twelve weeks we were not all better, but we had all of the tools that we needed to get all better. We continued to use the tools for weeks and months and I'd like to tell you that we got better quick, but it actually took us about two years to get to where we needed to be. That might seem like a long time, until you consider the fact that that was about 17 years ago. So two years now seems like a drop in the bucket and certainly worth all of the healthy years of marriage that we've enjoyed since then. Our children have also been able to grow up in a house with their biological mom and biological dad present.

So, I know things may seem really tough for you. I'm

sure that they are, but I want to encourage you to put your trust not in a person, not in a book, but in God's truth, and trust God to transform your marriage just like He did mine.

This book is part of a twelve-week intensive marriage program called "The Marriage Miracle" that is saving marriages all across the nation.

Discover the whole experience at:

TheMarriageMiracle.com

Chapter One

A Better Understanding of Your Spouse

A good place to start building a solid marriage is an understanding of the origin of marriage. For this we will look to Genesis 2:21-24:

> *"So the Lord God caused a deep sleep to fall on Adam, and he slept; and He took one of his ribs, and closed up the flesh in its place. Then the rib which the Lord God had taken from man He made into a woman, and He brought her to the man. And Adam said: 'This is now bone of my bones and flesh of my flesh; she shall be called Woman, because she was taken out of Man. 'For this reason a man shall leave his father and mother and be joined to his wife, and they shall become one flesh."*

Now I know we have heard that scripture many times, but it's important to get that picture image in your mind; <u>man was originally created as one being</u>. My personal understanding of the word *man* in that passage is not gender specific, it's more like the word we use today *mankind*. Man was made *one flesh* and then God said, *"It is not good for him to be alone, so I'm going to make him a helper…"* He then takes something out of *man* and creates his counterpart; *woman*.

But notice the verse that says, *"For this reason a man shall leave his father and mother and be joined to his wife."* That is a scripture verse that many of us had spoken at our weddings. But do we ever stop and really think about the *reason* this verse is referring to? The *reason* is this: man was originally one—and then from one—God made them two unique individual beings. Even though there are distinct differences between the two halves, marriage joins them back together into *one flesh.*

It is fascinating to know that men and women are different physically, mentally, emotionally and spiritually. However, God designed us to function as one. It is equally interesting that the differences that God has established are the very things that Satan uses to frustrate us about our spouse. Isn't that the case most of the time?

We get frustrated with our spouses because they are not acting like us; they're not doing what we would do; they're not saying what we think should be said at the moment. The way the devil accomplishes this is by confusing our understandings of male/female differences. Therefore, we must identify and understand the unique differences between males and females.

I'm going to give you two corresponding lists: one of male characteristics and one of female characteristics. First let me say that these are not accurate of all men and women, but I'm sure you will get the point.

Male/Female Differences

Male	**Female**
Left brain/logic	Right brain/emotion
Focused on achievement	Focused on relationships
12,000 words per day	25,000 words per day
Tough and strong	Tender and gentle
Talks to convey solutions	Talks to expand relationships
Risk-takers	Security and order
Look for long-haul	Concerned about the present
More compartmentalized	More connected
Value freedom and space	Hate aloneness
Objective	Subjective
Deal in generalities	Deal in details

I have heard it put this way about the difference between the way men and women think and communicate: our brains are like a collection of boxes. If a man is going to shift from one box to another, he must close that box and move to the other, and forget about the previous one. However, a woman can talk from one box and think about how it's going to affect another box which is going to affect another box and so forth! It's almost as though their boxes are connected with a spaghetti-like network. Simply put, men and women think and communicate very differently.

Understanding this contrast is vital to a healthy marriage. Instead of getting frustrated, the next time your spouse does something you do not understand, realize that this is the way God wired him or her. He intentionally made your mate different from you. So, where you are weak—your spouse is probably going to be strong; where your spouse is weak—you are probably going to be strong and the two of you—together—complete each other.

Proper Hierarchy of Priorities

The next step in building a solid marriage is a firm foundation of priorities. If your priorities are not in order, every decision you make will be subject to challenges. The following is a healthy hierarchy of priorities and you would do well to memorize them. This is one of those things that appear to be so simple, but when you read the list many are going to think, *"Yea Paul, I understand that,"* but the truth is they get out of order easily. You don't intentionally re-prioritize them, but life does it for you.

Let's go through the list:

1. God
2. Spouse
3. Children
4. Job/ministry
5. Extended family
6. Hobbies & interests

Often when I recite this list, I will see a look of frustration on either the wife's or husband's face. For example, if the husband is a fisherman he'll think, *"Great, I'm never going to get to go fishing again, because it's at the bottom of the list!"* But that is not true. The truth is that if the man has these priorities in order, he will be able to go fishing and when he goes, he will be able to go guilt free.

We counseled a couple years ago and when I asked the wife what her hierarchy of priorities was she replied very quickly, *"God, my parents, my children and my spouse."* She thought that order was perfectly fine because they were all in the top four, but from the outside looking in we could easily identify that many of their problems were the result of that list being out of order.

No one would intentionally move his or her job from position four up to position two, but again we don't have to do it intentionally; life will do it for you. It happened to me years ago. I felt like it was so important to provide for my family that, for a season, I worked a full time job and two part time jobs. I thought I was doing a good thing, but the end result was that my job had become a higher priority than my spouse and my children. In time, important things got neglected and there were problems.

I have never personally experienced conflict from extended family but we have counseled many, many couples who have. If you're not careful it can become especially difficult because you will feel like you are being told to choose between your spouse, your mom and dad or one of your siblings. None of these things are necessary if you establish a proper hierarchy of priorities. I'm not asking you to cut off other relationships, I'm just asking you to put them in order.

For instance, let's say that I had promised to take my wife Evie out for a date on a particular Friday night. My brother calls and says, *"Hey, we would like to go and do something with you guys on Friday night."* I would tell my brother, *"You know I would really love to do that with you guys, but I promised Evie a date that night and I want to stick with it, so how about we get together on Saturday night, or the following Friday?"* I would do this so my priorities would be kept in order.

Modeling this proper hierarchy of priorities in front of

your children will teach them how a man should treat his wife and how a woman should prioritize her husband. When priorities are in order—things go very well.

Hearing from God

So, we know that God is our creator and that He is our number one priority. Therefore, we must look to Him for help. I want to share with you now about the importance of hearing from God. <u>If you are not hearing from God, you won't be open to change.</u>

Now this point is huge; you've got to be open to hearing from the Lord, otherwise you won't apply the things you learn in this book because they won't be real to you. Two church services a week is not enough, you need to hear from God *daily*.

The Book of Matthew, records the time when Jesus was tempted by the devil:

> *"Now when the tempter came to Him, he said, 'If you are the Son of God, command that these stones become bread.' But He answered and said, 'It is written, 'Man shall not live by bread alone, but by every word that proceeds from the mouth of God.'" (Matthew 4:3—4)*

The word *proceeds* in this scripture means *continually flowing*. Yes, we have the Word of God in the form of the Bible—

which is called the Logos Word, but there is something called the Rhema Word which simply means, *God's Word communicated to us through prayer.* God is speaking to us every day, and we've got to get connected to that supply of wisdom on a daily basis.

Another interesting fact concerning this scripture is that, even though Satan clearly knew *who* Jesus was (remember: Satan spent millennia in heaven before he was cast down to the earth), he does not greet Jesus by saying, *"Hello, Son of God."* What does he say? *"IF you are the Son of God..."* That is Satan's modus operandi; he is forever spinning the truth—trying his best to get us to question God.

How does Jesus respond? *"Man shall not live by bread alone but by every word that proceeds from the mouth of God."* Two interesting things about that statement are number one, Jesus didn't respond with His own words—He's quoting Old Testament scripture (Deuteronomy 8:3) which tells us that <u>Jesus studied and memorized scripture</u> and secondly, it tells us that <u>even Jesus had to talk to His Heavenly Father on a daily basis</u>. Many Bible scholars believe that Jesus got up and prayed for three hours every morning—and yet we try to survive on three minutes per day! If Jesus needed three hours, who are we to think we can get by on three minutes?

Again, this was being said when Jesus was being tempted and He said that there is *bread* for the body but there is

Word for the spirit. Bread keeps my physical body strong but this daily Word from my Heavenly Father keeps my *spirit* strong. So how can you get every word that proceeds from the mouth of God? You've got to do three things:

1. Study Scripture

The first is to study scripture, God's written Word. Some people will read this and think, *"I read my scripture ... I do my two chapters a day."* But I'm not talking about a religious act to get your brownie points for the day. I'm talking about devouring scripture in large quantities to the extent that you are getting loads of truth downloaded into your mind on a daily basis.

I suggest two ways of studying scripture: one is by studying *a particular book*. Let's say that you took the Book of James and, instead of just reading it, you really studied it; you found out everything about the Book of James by using online commentaries—things like: What time in history was it written? To whom was James writing? What were they going through? Learning all those things causes the story to come alive. It's almost like watching a movie; you become so engrossed in it that you actually want to pick up the book and read it every day.

The second way is by studying *a particular person* in scripture. For example, studying the life of the prophet Samuel will take you through several books of the Old Testament. It will be easy to read because it is unfolding in a story.

As you read scripture, godly principles will be stored in your mind that will lead and guide you in life. The Word will literally come alive in you.

2. Daily Prayer

Second, is daily prayer; God's *continual word* for each and every day. Let me give you an example of this. Let's say that you plan to discuss some important things with your spouse tonight when you get home at 6 o'clock. You need wisdom and very specific direction for that conversation and you will only get that wisdom through prayer.

James 1:5 says, *"If any of you lacks wisdom, let him ask of God, who gives to all liberally and without reproach, and it will be given to him."* *Without reproach* simply means you don't have to be concerned about how many times you ask. I ask for wisdom in my morning prayer and in my evening prayer. I know that I ask for wisdom several times throughout the day because I need His daily wisdom on how to guide my conversations, my meetings and my decisions.

3. Journaling

The third is journaling. I know that some people don't like to journal and I find that it's especially difficult for men. I had a problem with journaling years ago because I viewed it as something a girl would do, such as keeping a diary, until I ended up in a program that forced me to journal. As I wrote, I began to see the value of journaling and I have continued the practice to this day. I like to put it this way; the only thing worse than *not* getting a word from God is *getting* a word from God and *forgetting* it!

When you pray, ask God for help and then write down what you feel He is saying to you. *"Today I got nothing"* is a valid journal entry, but most of the time you will have something substantial to write and as you look back over the days of notes, you will see an answer beginning to surface.

Losing Your Thirst for Selfishness

When you connect with *every word that proceeds from the mouth of God*, your thirst for selfishness will begin to diminish, and, as you will see in the chapters that follow, the majority of marriage problems are rooted in selfishness.

There is a story in John chapter 4 about a woman at a well, and the story line goes like this: Jesus was traveling with His disciples through Samaria, and while His disciples went to get some food, He sat near a well to rest. While sitting there, a Samaritan woman came to draw water from the well, and Jesus asked her for a drink of water—which was pretty shocking because the racial tension between Jews and Samaritans was fierce. The woman began to tell Jesus how she comes to this well, draws out water, and takes it back to her little village every day. When the supply diminishes, she comes back to the well the next day and draws water once again.

Read this story too fast and you'll miss the whole thing. Study it slowly like I'm encouraging you to study scripture and you will find out that <u>Jesus is drawing a parallel between the woman's thirst for the water in this well—and her thirst for an emotional need that had gone unmet.</u> Jesus goes on to say:

> *"Whoever drinks of this water will thirst again, but whoever drinks of the water that I shall give him will never thirst. But the water that I shall give him will become in him a fountain of water springing up into everlasting life."* The woman said to Him, *"Sir, give me this water, that I may not thirst, nor come here to draw."* (John 4:13—15)

Jesus responded, *"Go, call your husband, and come here."* Now that would seem like a random statement until you realize that Jesus was telling her to go get the *water* (i.e., her man) she was currently drinking to satisfy her thirst.

The woman replies; *"Oh I don't have a husband."* And Jesus says, *"You're right, you don't have a husband, you've had five and the one that you have now is not your husband."* (In a more modern day translation I would say, the word *boyfriends* might fit there.)

What Jesus was saying to the woman is this: "At some point in your life you had emotional needs for affection and sexual fulfillment and you reached out to a well—a man to fulfill that need, and you did it the wrong way. You got the first boyfriend and that relationship lasted for a while, but when that one ran its course, you got thirsty for another one, and you came back and found boyfriend number two. When that relationship ran its course you were thirsty again and found boyfriend number three, four, and five. Now, you're on boyfriend number six and guess what? When this relationship runs its course, you're going to be thirsty once again, just like you are every day for more water from this well."

In her carnal mind the woman is blown away by the fact that this man had some kind of water that could quench her physical thirst forever. That's not at all what Jesus was saying. He was telling her that He had living water called *Truth,* and if she drank from this well of truth, she would never thirst for the selfish things that were destroying her life again.

So, let me connect the two stories: *living by every word that proceeds from the mouth of God* and this story about *the woman at the well*. The *living water* that Jesus told the woman at the well about *is* every word that proceeds from the mouth of God.

Now here's something very interesting: remember; the word *proceeds* in Matthew 4:4 means *continually flowing*—right? Well guess what the word *drinks* in John 4:14 means… are you ready for this? It means *continually drinking*.

Isn't that something? Jesus is telling us that—in order to have the best possible life—we should be *continually drinking* every Word that is *continually flowing* from our Heavenly Father. Apply this spiritual truth to your marriage and you will be amazed at the difference it makes.

You and your spouse must tap into that well on a daily basis and begin to drink from the truth, the knowledge and wisdom that God will give you. The more you drink from that well on a daily basis, the less you will thirst for selfishness—it will actually begin to diminish and go away. So, if you pray, study scripture and journal on a daily basis, you will slowly but surely lose your thirst for the things that are destroying your marriage. As you begin to do these three things, I encourage you to put on an attitude of peace towards your spouse and think the best of each other.

Chapter Two

Feelings and Communication Skills

When dealing with your spouse's feelings it is important to understand that <u>an emotion shared should elicit an emotional response</u>. So, in other words if your spouse comes to you and says something with any emotion behind it; whether it's anger, sadness, concern or joy, you should have an emotional response.

Some unproductive responses are:

> **Logic:** *"I don't know why you would see it that way…"*
> **Facts:** *"Well, let me tell you how it really is…"*
> **Reasons:** *"I can tell you why it's happening that way…"*
> **Criticism:** *"You shouldn't think that way, that's ridiculous…"*
> **Your own needs:** *"You think you had a bad day, you should hear about mine!"*
> **Neglect:** *"I just don't want to hear it; I don't have time for that right now…"*

Some productive responses are:

Understanding: *"I can see why you would feel that way; I'd probably feel the same..."*
Empathy: *"That happened to me one time and I was very frustrated too..."*
Gentleness: *"I care about you and how you're feeling..."*
Reassurance: *"Listen, this won't last forever, things will get better..."*

Acceptance

Romans 15:7 says, *"Therefore receive one another, just as Christ also received us, to the glory of God."* Just as Christ gave you the gift of acceptance, you in turn should give it to your spouse. It's like handing your spouse a gift, but it's very important to understand that *acceptance* and *approval* are two very different things.

Approval implies; *"What you're doing is okay with me."*

Acceptance implies; *"I take you the way you are."*

If you don't understand the distinct differences between these two words you will confuse the fact that you are *accepting* your spouse—as *approval* for what he or she is doing. For example, when a wife says to her husband, *"I can't accept you right now because of the way you're acting,"* she is probably saying, *"I don't approve of the way you are acting."* Here's a fact worth memorizing:

Acceptance comes BEFORE change.

Think about it; you won't change for someone that doesn't accept you. Why would you? If you're going to change and tomorrow the person you're changing for is going to bail on you, why go through all the trouble to change? This is a principle that is always true; acceptance comes before change.

This principle, by the way, is not only true in your marriage, but true in just about every other area of your life. It applies to your kids; if they do not feel accepted, they're not going to change. It applies to your job; if you have a co-worker that does not feel accepted by you; he is not going to willingly change anything for you.

Furthermore, it is vitally important to understand two things when it comes to acceptance:

1. You are not responsible for your spouse's behavior.

2. You are not responsible for your spouse's growth.

One of the things that fascinates me the most about God is that in His sovereign power He has the ability to break your will and make you do what He wants you to do—but He won't do it. He will never touch your will. And if God won't do it, who are you to think that you can break your spouse's will and make him or her grow or change his or her behavior? It's simply not going to happen.

The only way your spouse is going to change is when he or she decides to change. It must be a personal decision and not one coerced by someone else. All the preaching and arguing you've used to try to make your spouse change is of no effect. As a matter of fact, it actually drives him or her NOT to change—and possibly even causes your mate to dig his or her heels deeper into the dirt AGAINST the change. It's simply human nature.

Here's a great piece of advice:

You work on you and allow God to work on your spouse.

Communication

Communication is the free exchange of thoughts, ideas, opinions and feelings. It is open and honest and in it you become vulnerable, yet you know that you will remain committed to each other. (Again, that is based on acceptance.) The problem here is simple; you don't like to be open, honest and vulnerable. You may think, *"I don't want to become vulnerable because I'm afraid my spouse is going to say or do something that catches me off guard."* But good healthy communication is impossible without openness, honesty, and vulnerability.

Three Levels of Communication

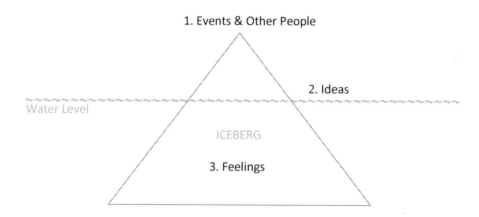

Most couples talk on the level of **events and other people** such as:

- *"How was your day?"*
- *"The kids need new tennis shoes."*
- *"Listen to what happened at the office today…"*

It's easy to talk about events and other people.

Some couples go to the deeper level of **ideas** – such as:

- Plans for the kid's college.
- What you believe about God.
- What you would like to do in your retirement years.

Ideas are a little more difficult to talk about.

But as you can see, the mass below the water line is the biggest part of the iceberg and that is the level of **feelings**. They may be the hardest to talk about, but <u>feelings are the most important level of communication</u>. You must get to the point where you can discuss your feelings with each other.

Feelings lead to behavior, so if you have a feeling inside, you are going to eventually act out on that feeling. That's not always bad; it actually works for good thoughts and good behavior as well. Therefore, it is very important that you are able to communicate your feelings clearly, so that your spouse fully understands them.

Communication Pitfalls

Here are seven communication pitfalls to avoid:

1. Absolutes
2. Gunny-sacking
3. Predicting reactions
4. Passive listening
5. Negative / Critical listening
6. Preaching
7. Nagging

Absolutes: The use of words such as *always* and *never*. Now, I have to admit this was very difficult for me; I had the tendency to use absolutes often. I would say *"You always nag me,"* or *"You always do this,"* and *"You never do that."* It was just a big part of my vocabulary and it caused a lot of problems. The reason why negative absolutes cause problems is because <u>they are rarely ever true</u> and they will instantly put your spouse on the defense.

Gunny-sacking: Quietly gathering offenses and allowing them to fester deep inside you. I had a tendency to do that too. I felt like I was being a good guy by not saying anything in the moment, but I was actually gathering evidence into my memory bank so that when I did finally blow up, I'd come across like a prosecuting attorney!

Predicting Reactions: When I say *this*, I know she's going to say *that* back to me, or when *this* happens I know she's going to respond like *that*. The problem with this approach is that we are often wrong.

Passive Listening: Again, I hate to tell all of my faults, but this was another great challenge for me. I often didn't really care what Evie was saying, so I would be like the old cartoon character with the newspaper in front of me saying, *"Uh huh, yes, uh huh,"* until Evie started asking me what she had just said to me and I didn't know! You might as well say, *"Due to lack of interest today has been cancelled!"* It's a terrible pitfall.

Negative or Critical Listening: A very common problem that often leads to impolite interrupting in an effort to challenge and/or critique what the other person is saying. We become critical when we feel our spouse is not thinking and communicating correctly.

Preaching: I may not even have to describe this one because the problems associated with preaching are so obvious. No one likes be preached at during a disagreement. It is actually considered didactic communication, which simply implies that you are attempting to teach or moralize the other person.

Nagging: Constantly trying to make your point—over and over again. In most cases, the more dominant spouse will resort to nagging but the results are rarely—if ever—positive.

L.I.V.E. Communication Technique

If you would like a better way to communicate, I have a great technique for you. I call it the *L.I.V.E. Communication Technique.*

    Listen—carefully
    Interpret—what you heard
    Validate—with empathy
    Express—your feelings

Listen carefully: The first step in this technique is to listen to your spouse carefully. This may seem like an easy thing to do but it is actually very difficult. It was a challenge for me because I don't think fast on my feet. So, when Evie was talking to me, half of my brain was listening to her, but the other half was thinking ahead of what I was going to say next!

Listening carefully means that you shut down everything else in your mind and focus intently on what your spouse is saying.

Simply put; people do not talk because they want to fill the room with hot air—they talk because they **desperately want to be heard**.

I once heard of a study that suggests that the brain secretes the same chemicals when a person is being listened to as it does when he or she feels loved. In other words, being listened to and being loved are so similar—the brain can't tell the difference.

Interpret what you heard: After you have listened carefully and heard everything that your spouse is saying, interpret back what you heard him or her say. It doesn't have to be a point-by-point rehearsal—just say it back in a few sentences; *"What I heard you say is…"* and go on to repeat the highlights for clarity.

This step has several positive side effects. First, it produces *warm fuzzies* in your spouse because you not only listened carefully to every word—you took the time to make sure you heard him or her correctly. Next, it gives your spouse the opportunity to either say, *"Yes, you got it right"* or, *"You got the first half right, but the second half is not what I meant to say."* If it is the latter, respond with something like, *"Okay, please tell me that part again because I really want to understand."* <u>Do not move on until you clearly understand everything your spouse said</u>.

Validate with empathy: Validating implies, *"You are not crazy... your thoughts and feelings are valid."* Empathy simply implies, *"I can see why you would feel that way."* To validate with empathy, say something like, *"You know—if that happened to me, I'd probably be upset too."*

Here's the great challenge to this step: we think that if you empathize with your spouse and validate his or her feelings—it will come across as though you are agreeing with what he or she just said. However, people that are emotionally mature will have the ability to empathize, even though they don't agree with every point their spouse made. You could even say something like, *"Even though I don't agree with every point you just made, I have to admit; if that was me and I had those thoughts, I would be terribly upset."* So, empathizing with your spouse and validating his or her feelings is very healthy. It indicates that you understand where he or she is coming from.

Express your feelings: Now it's your turn to talk and your spouse is going to switch to the "L" position and listen carefully. Continue to circle through this pattern until you clearly understand each other and come to a *win/win* conclusion.

Someone recently pointed out to me that the L.I.V.E. technique done backwards is E.V.I.L! So be sure to use this technique properly and you will see great results. And by the way, this technique works well—not only in your marriage—

but in every area of your life; with your children, your coworkers, and your friends—anyone with whom you communicate. The technique will feel mechanical in the beginning but press through the awkwardness until you begin to see the positive results. Use it long enough and it will become a normal way of communicating. In time, you will probably notice people saying things to you like, *"I love talking to you ... you're a great listener and seem to always understand where I'm coming from."*

Use the L.I.V.E. Communication Technique as often as you can and trust God to transform the communication of your marriage.

Chapter Three
Understanding and Expressing Anger

Anger. Everybody deals with anger. Did you know that God gets angry? Psalms 7:11 says that *"He is angry at the wicked every day,"* so God gets angry. Did you know that Jesus got angry? Do you remember the story about when He drove the money changers out of the temple? He turned over tables; He was definitely angry. So, if God gets angry and Jesus gets angry, then being angry is not a sin.

The apostle Paul tells us in Ephesians 4:26 *"Be angry and sin not,"* so it is apparently possible to be angry in a way that doesn't cause us to sin—but it is very, very difficult! So that is why Paul goes on in Ephesians and Colossians to tell us to put anger far away from us. In other words, try and put as much distance between yourself and anger as you possibly can. The problem is not anger; <u>the problem is the root of anger</u>.

I'm about to give you a theory and it's probably one of the most powerful theories that has impacted my life. It's a theory about anger, and it says this:

The root of anger is a blocked goal.

I can remember the first time I heard that, my first thought was, *"That can't be—anger is too big of a problem to put into that small of a box,"* but I can tell you that after 17 years of applying it, this is a principle that is true every single time; the root of anger is a blocked goal.

So, now let me break down the concept of a blocked goal. Let's say that I think things should go a certain way, but they're not going that way (my goal is being blocked) and that stirs up an emotion inside of me that we call *anger*.

This theory has a second part which says:

The person or thing that blocked my goal is the target of my anger.

Think about this and you'll see how accurate it is; every time you get angry, the person or thing that blocked your goal becomes the target of your anger.

For example, let's say that I am going to paint the walls in my brand new office, and I'm looking through a magazine and happen to see a picture of an executive standing in his office which has cobalt blue walls. I'm thinking, *"Wow, I really want to project the same executive image, so I'm going to paint my office walls cobalt blue!"* It's silly but it's important to me.

Just as I make that decision, my wife walks in the room

and says, *"Oh you're going to paint your office? You should paint the walls red."* The fact that I already feel like she's too controlling and pushes her way on me causes my goal to get blocked really quick. I'm thinking, *"She's going to force me to paint these walls red"* and I get very angry.

Now, the way society had taught me to handle a situation like this was to suppress the other person's opinion so that mine would win. And because I had a bend towards sarcasm, I would say something to her like, *"Red, are you serious? Where did you get your design skills from, a third grader?"* And of course if someone else had been in the room when I said that, she would be furious! As a matter of fact, when the other person left the room, she would look at me and say something like, *"How dare you talk to me like that in front of other people?"* Well now she's angry—and guess what her blocked goal is; she would like to appear to others to be an intelligent person, but I've just blocked that goal by making her sound like an idiot, so now she's angry with me!

Now we're arguing back and forth, I'm saying *"Look, you're a control freak—you come in here telling me what to do. I wanted a cobalt blue office and you're saying I have to paint it red!"* And she argues back, *"I am NOT a control freak … if there's a freak in this room buddy—it's you!"* and we start this whole new argument that quickly spins out of control.

This is what I call a SURFACE LEVEL ARGUMENT and they can last for days, weeks, and even years. Remember this:

> *Surface level arguments are distractions that keep you from addressing the real root of the problem.*

Here's another example; let's say that you're in traffic and you want to change lanes; you check your mirrors and start to veer over when all of a sudden you hear a horn honk; you quickly swerve back into your original lane and you say *"Wow I didn't see that guy."* But the next thing you know the guy is pulling up next to you, rolling down his window, and he's screaming at the top of his lungs, the veins are coming out in his neck, he's giving you the sign that he thinks you're number one, and you think he's going to actually crash into you just to make his point!

Here's the question: Where did his anger come from? What is that guy's blocked goal? Think about it for a minute.

There are many theories that could explain why a guy would become so angry, but here is what I think; the guy may have been brought up by a father who had very strong and possibly even militaristic disciplines. When his dad punished him he may have insisted, *"You're wrong, you're wrong, you're wrong—even when you think you're right—you're wrong!"* He heard that for 18, maybe 20 years, and then he finally gets out on his own and he thinks, *"Now nobody is going to tell me that I'm wrong ... nobody is going to do me wrong ... you don't do me wrong!"* Now he's in traffic and you accidentally start to cut him off and instantly—20 years of anger and frustration rise to the surface and he begins to honk his horn and scream at you.

Anger is a powerful thing and if you don't know how to get to the root of it, you'll never overcome it. Again, the root of anger is a blocked goal and the person or thing that blocked your goal will be the target of your anger. It's extremely important to learn to identify the root of anger.

This theory of anger works—not only in your marriage—it works in every area of life. When my children would get angry, I could get to their blocked goal and resolve the issue quickly. For example, when my son Alex was younger, he exercised his macho muscles and addressed me with an angry tone. My old way of handling that would have been raising my voice louder than his and saying, *"Oh no—you don't talk to me that way young man! You go to your room and I'll be in there in a few minutes to give you a spanking!"* My new way of handling it would be to say something like, *"Hey, wait a minute Alex; tell daddy what's not going like you think it should be going."* (Because he would not have known what the term *blocked goal* meant, I asked the same thing in terms he could understand.) It may have taken a little coaching, but he would eventually tell me what was really causing his anger, and I could get to the root of it and resolve it. By the way, that does not mean that I allowed disrespect; I dealt with that separately, but as you can see; this method is very effective with children.

Additionally, this method of handling anger will work for you on the job. For example, let's say that I'm in a committee meeting and someone, let's call him *Bob*, is obviously getting angry and complicating things. As chair of the committee, my old way of handling that situation would have probably been to out-vote the guy! But I learned to say, *"Hey Bob, what's not going like you think it should—what's got you upset about this?"* And as he would begin to express his feelings, I would be able to address the real problem and probably do it in a way that would win his vote. This theory works in every area of life, so learn to identify the root of anger.

Learn to Identify the Root of the Anger

I want to give you another example that illustrates this method in the context of marriage:

A wife goes out to her mailbox, opens it, and finds a cancellation notice from the electric company. She walks back into the house and yells at her husband, *"I'm sick and tired of never being able to pay our bills."* The husband yells back, *"Well, why do you always put it on me? You pay the bills, and all you ever do is nag, nag, nag!"* And then they banter back and forth, *"No I don't!" "Yes you do!"* And then she yells at him, *"Well, all you ever do is lie around and watch TV, why don't you get a better paying job?"*

So, we've got two angry people here, wouldn't you agree? Well let's see if we can identify the root of their anger. The wife: she's just a mean old woman looking for a fight, right? No, probably not. Women have a built in need for security, it's just part of their nature. If you remember in chapter one, we talked about the way that God made us. We started out as one whole flesh; God took woman from man and made us two distinct halves, and made us distinctly different. Well one of the distinct differences about a female is the need for security; it's a good instinct because it makes sure that she takes care of herself and her babies. Therefore, security is very important to women.

So, a cancellation notice means that the lights are going to go out, and let's say that they have an electric stove, the stove is not going to work. Guess what that means? That means she can't heat the baby's bottles or cook the food that they need. She begins to connect the dots and it quickly blocks her goal for security.

Now let's take a look at the husband: He's just a bully looking to take somebody's head off, right? No, the truth is he's actually a good guy that has just gotten very angry. Men have a built in need for affirmation. I can relate to this because I'm a man, and I know how important it is for me to feel like I'm doing a good job as the provider for my home. Years ago, I was working like crazy with one full time job and two part time jobs but we were still coming up short paying our bills. I felt like I was doing everything I possibly could to be a good provider and if Evie said something like this to me, it emasculated me. It made me feel like less of a man and that I was not taking good care of my wife and my kids. So, the goal that is being blocked for the husband in this example is his goal for affirmation.

Here is a fact that you should remember:

Surface level arguments rarely address the true root of anger.

In the case of this couple, the surface level arguments are things like, *"I'm sick and tired of never being able to pay our bills"* and, *"Why do you put it on me, you always pay the bills!"* Those are the surface level aspects of the argument and they simply do not address the true root of each spouse's anger.

Until you identify the root of anger you will never properly address it. Stop and think for a minute; how many surface level arguments have you had that kept you stirred up with details that never really addressed the true root of the anger? I know there have been many—and they've probably been over silly little things. After years of counseling couples, I can tell you that the majority of the arguments that happen in marriages are over silly little things; they are rarely over something really big. Couples don't come in to my office and say, *"I just found out my husband has been out at night robbing banks!"* I don't hear problems like that. I hear silly little problems like, *"We were heading out and we had to stop by Home Depot and he said, 'you know it's going to take 10 minutes to get there,' and I said 'no way, it's going to take a good 20 minutes,'"* and they end up in this crazy, totally unproductive, surface level argument. So you are not alone; the great majority of marital arguments are over the smallest, silliest little things.

So here is your exercise for this principle: whenever you or your spouse—or anybody else for that matter—is angry; stop and ask them, **"What is not going the way you think it should?"** If they are like me, they may need a few minutes to figure out the answer to that question because it's common to be angry and not even know why.

Resolving Conflicts

Now that you know how to get to the root of anger, the next step is learning how to resolve conflicts which leads us to another important principle:

To resolve conflicts you must use 'feelings words,' and eliminate absolutes.

This is one of those things that is easy to say but very, very hard to do. I personally had a problem with the whole *feelings* thing because I viewed it as a girl thing; girls talk about their feelings, men talk about logical things. I would say, *"I don't need to tell you how I feel about this, I'm going to tell you what I know about this—this is the way it is!"* It took a lot of intentional effort for me to get to the place where I could easily express my true feelings. In time, I discovered that this method actually worked in my favor; I got the results I had been hoping for all along.

Ridding my vocabulary of negative absolutes was one of the most difficult things I've ever done. They came very naturally to me. It was my knee-jerk reaction to say things like, *"You ALWAYS do this…"* and, *"You NEVER do that…"* The problem with absolutes is that they are rarely—if ever—true. Because they are not true, they will cause your spouse to go immediately into defense mode—and the fight is on! Therefore, you too must rid your vocabulary of negative absolutes.

Let's go back to the argument between our lovely sweethearts and see if we can identify the absolutes in their disagreement. The wife says, *"I'm sick and tired of never being able to pay our bills."* What is the absolute there? The word *never.* Is it true that they NEVER pay their bills? No, it's probably not. The truth is that they pay a lot of their bills, but, for whatever reason, the electric bill kept getting put off until they got a cancellation notice. So *never being able to pay our bills* is not a truthful statement which caused her husband to go into defense mode.

Now, let's look for absolutes in the husband's response: *"Well, why do you always put it on me? You pay the bills and all you ever do is nag, nag, nag."* Do you see them? The first one is *always.* Do you think she ALWAYS puts it on him? No, she probably tries to figure it out sometimes on her own. The next two are *all* and *ever.* Is nagging her husband ALL this woman does EVERY waking hour of the day? No, it's not true, so of course, she's going to instantly defend that. Then she yells back at him, *"Well all you ever do is lie around and watch TV!"* What are the absolutes here? *All* and *ever.* These words come out of our mouth so quickly, but they are so problematic because they are not true. Do you really think this guy lies around and watches television from the time he gets up until the time he goes to bed? No, he probably goes to work every day and does many chores around the house when he is home. So, when he hears a statement like that, of course, he's going to take offense to it, and say that it's not true.

Proverbs 15:1 says, *"A soft answer turns away wrath, but grievous words stir up anger."* Absolutes in a disagreement are grievous words. So, remember this:

Absolutes can be argued forever and never resolved.

Yes, I know I used an absolute in that statement, but it's true! To help you remember this important fact, let me give you a metaphor—a visual image of what absolutes do. Let's say that you're running and you have a bag on your back filled with little logs, and as you run, you reach back and grab one of the logs and throw it out in the path in front of you, and then you trip over it. You may be thinking, *"Who in the world would do that?"* Answer: <u>anyone who uses absolutes in their communication</u>. That's the picture image you should have; *"Every time I throw out an absolute, I'm going to trip over it!"*

Feelings Words

By now, you may be thinking, *"If I can't use absolutes, what can I use?"* The answer is *feelings words*. How do you do that? Well, let's revisit the argument between our lovely sweethearts once again for specific examples:

The wife goes to the mail box and gets the cancellation

notice, she freaks out on her husband which makes him very angry, BUT THIS TIME the husband identifies the root of his anger—his blocked goal—and he responds with *feelings words* by saying, *"Honey, listen, when you say things like that, it makes me feel like you don't trust me to take care of you and the kids."*

Now, I should tell you at this point that this argument example is not hypothetical—it is based on an actual argument that Evie and I had about 17 years ago when our marriage was terribly messed up. My old way was to throw out sarcasm and absolutes, and it would turn into a surface level argument that would last for days and maybe even weeks. Then I learned this technique and I was able to stop myself before I responded (which is a challenge in and of itself!), then I would say to myself, *"Alright, I know I'm angry… I feel my blood pressure rising, the hair is standing up on the back of my neck—I am definitely angry!"* Then I would ask myself, *"What is my blocked goal?"* After giving it some serious thought, I answered by saying, *"When you say things like that it makes me feel like you don't trust me to take care of you and the kids,"* and she responded, *"Oh, Paul, I DO trust you to take care of us, but every time one of these notices come in I feel scared,"* which then helped me understand that her blocked goal was her need for security.

That day we went on to affirm each other's feelings and as we talked things out in a healthy way, we discovered the REAL root of our problem: <u>we had no control over our finances</u>!

That revelation led to us taking a Christian financial class and learning how to budget our money properly. The end result was no more financial crises and no more cancellation notices.

Anger-fueled surface-level arguments can last for days and are completely ineffective, but when you resolve the real root of anger, all of those surface level issues begin to fade away.

You really can conquer anger—yours and your spouse's—by simply applying the concepts and techniques described in this chapter.

Chapter Four
Emotional Maturity

Emotional maturity is the ability to override a conscious mental reaction to either circumstances or the actions of another person. Simply put, it is the ability to suppress selfishness and act wisely. That is easier said than done.

Emotional maturity is controlled by a conscious decision: you make the choice to be either emotionally mature or emotionally immature. It's kind of like a switch deep down inside you over which you have complete control to turn *On* or *Off*. That switch stays in the *On* position when you are in public and other people are watching, but you often turn it *Off* when you're with your spouse. Amazingly, you are more emotionally mature with a cashier that you don't even know, than you are with your spouse who means more to you than anyone else in the world.

Why would you allow your emotional maturity switch to be flipped into the *Off* position when you are at home? Because you have a high level of familiarity with your spouse and, like a child, you know you can get away with demanding your own way. The truth of the matter is that it takes a lot of emotional maturity to say and do the right thing.

In chapter 3 you learned that the root of anger is a blocked goal. You also learned that once you identify what that blocked goal is, you should express it to your spouse using *feelings words*. In this chapter you will learn the importance of emotional maturity by doing a quick emotional maturity assessment.

The following are examples of emotional maturity levels at various ages in life.

Age 2: Crying, screaming, and tantrums.

Age 10: Yelling, rebellion, pouting, defiance, and an inability to reason.

Age 15: Interrupting, silent treatment, name-calling, one-upping, and creative revenge.

Age 20: Outwardly mature but inwardly resentful and scheming retaliation.

Age 25: Able to suppress selfishness and act wisely.

You may be thinking that not every 25 year old acts that way—and I would agree; there are 50 year olds that don't even act that way, but the point of this scale is to show the different levels of emotional maturity—or lack thereof—at various ages of life.

When it comes to your level of emotional maturity during conflict with your spouse, based on that scale—what is your relative age? Take a minute to answer that question and be honest with yourself.

Once you marry and launch into society you are considered to be mature adults by most people's standards. You have mature bodies, you work mature jobs, you have many mature responsibilities such as buying a car, a home, clothing, food, and making a wide variety of mature daily decisions. You are considered adults, able to maintain your maturity in public but something very interesting happens when you deal with adversity in the privacy of your own home: you resort to the emotional maturity of a child! Isn't that interesting? Somehow you reach inside and flip that switch that has been *On* all day at work—*Off*.

Just as an immature child screams, *"It's my turn, you've had two turns and now it's my turn!"* You simply cannot resist the temptation to yell, interrupt and demand your way. In the moment your knee-jerk reaction is to flip the switch *Off* and revert to the emotional maturity level of a ten year old.

The end result is that you say things that seriously damage your relationships. A husband or wife will often go back and say, *"I'm sorry for what I said ... I didn't mean it and I shouldn't have said that,"* and try to take the hurtful words back.

That is a noble thing to do if you've said something wrong, but it is almost impossible to erase the damage caused by hurtful words. The more you repeat the immature tantrum, the more your spouse resents you and avoids communication with you. Over time, it becomes a learned reactive behavior.

Even worse is when the other spouse responds with the same immature tantrum. Now that's a sight to behold; when a couple really has a knock-down drag-out! I've had couples go totally ballistic while sitting on the couch in my office during a counseling session! Two very mature, highly educated, emotionally mature people reach inside and flip that switch *Off*—and go at it like a couple of ten year old spoiled brats! It's an amazing phenomenon to me; something that they would never allow to happen in the general public, but when it's with their spouse and they know they can get away with it … buddy, the fight is on!

The following is an example of the difference between emotional immaturity and emotional maturity. It's very important that you get this concept of emotional maturity, so I'm going to give you first an example of emotional immaturity.

Example of Emotional Immaturity

A husband and wife have a disagreement that gets out of hand. The husband raises his voice with every rebuttal and begins to swear and call his wife demeaning names. He eventually walks away refusing to resolve the issue.

That night, when the two of them go to bed, the husband, who is normally very affectionate, refuses to touch his wife even though he knows her love language is physical touch. It is as though he has built an invisible wall down the center of the bed; he's not going to even so much as touch her. He is withholding her desired affection in order to punish her for not giving in to his argument. Is he thinking, *"I'm going to punish her this way,"*? Probably not, but subliminally that's what is happening. It's just another way for him to communicate; *"You were wrong!"*

Here are the results of his actions:

- The wife loses respect for her husband.
- She is emotionally scarred by his name calling.
- She feels as though he doesn't care about her feelings.
- She begins to resent him, and…
- She begins to associate negative feelings with going to bed with him.

<u>We humans naturally return to pleasure and avoid pain</u>. If you associate your spouse with good feelings, you want to be

with him or her. If you associate your spouse with bad feelings, you want to avoid him or her. So, because of this treatment at night, the wife in our example begins to associate negative feelings with going to bed with her husband. And because of his emotional immaturity, the husband loses the respect of his wife and undermines his leadership in their home. In effect, his emotional immaturity has sabotaged his own goals simply because of his inability to be emotionally mature.

Example of Emotional Maturity

A husband and wife have a disagreement that starts to get out of hand. The husband lowers his voice, identifies the root of his and his wife's anger, and begins to use the L.I.V.E. Communication Technique to talk it out. That's a tough thing to do when the heat is on and emotions are raging, but he demands of himself to be emotionally mature. In essence, he's saying, *"Let's handle this in the right and productive way."*

That night when the two of them go to bed, the husband cuddles his wife even though he's still a little bit upset about the disagreement—he doesn't withhold his affection from his wife. He is confident that his views were clearly communicated in their talk and that giving her the affection she desires does not negate his stand on the issues they discussed.

Giving her the affection that she desires is another way to communicate to her; *"Even though we disagree, I still love you; I accept you and I will always be here for you."* That takes a lot of emotional maturity and determination to do the right thing.

Here are the results of his actions:

- The wife increases in respect for her husband.
- Something deep down inside her says, *"This man takes care of me, he loves me even when he disagrees with me, even when he's upset with me; he's always there for me."*
- She is emotionally comforted by his affection and willingness to work things out.
- She feels as though he genuinely cares about her feelings.
- She associates positive feelings with going to bed with him, and…
- She reasons, *"No matter what happens, at the end of the day; my husband will always be there for me."*

Because of his emotional maturity, the husband maintains respect from his wife and strengthens his leadership role in their home. In effect, he reaches his desired goals because of his ability to remain emotionally mature.

Those two examples clarify the difference that emotional maturity can make in a marriage.

King Solomon, whom God called the wisest man of all, had much to say about emotional maturity. Here are a few of his Proverbs concerning this topic:

- *"The heart of the righteous studies how to answer but the mouth of the wicked pours forth evil." (Proverbs 15:28)*

  Doesn't that second part sound like somebody that is emotionally immature? They can't resist; their mouth pours forth evil; ugly names, hard statements and absolutes.

- *"He who has understanding spares his words and a man of understanding is of a calm spirit." (Proverbs 17:27)*

  So if you have understanding and wisdom; you might say, *emotional maturity,* you're going to spare your words and have a calm spirit.

- *"Even a fool when he holds his peace is counted wise, that he shuts his lips he's esteemed as a man of understanding." (Proverbs 17:28)*

  In other words, if you can't think of something emotionally mature to say, just close your lips and say nothing! Your chances of being esteemed wise and a person of understanding are greater if you simply don't say a word! Now I'm not talking about giving your spouse the silent treatment, we've been through all of that, we know that that's not healthy. I'm just saying; when immaturity kicks in and the ugly words start to shoot out your mouth, have the wisdom to hold your tongue.

- *"The discretion of a man makes him slow to anger and his glory is to overlook a transgression." (Proverbs 19:11)*

Listen, I would recommend that all of us get used to taking wrong from time to time. Even when you're not wrong, just get used to saying; *"Okay, I'll take bad on that one."* Safely, 90% of marital arguments are not over huge things, they're over small, little bitty things like how long it's going to take to get to the restaurant – or who strapped the car seat in last; *"It's not strapped in properly … it was you!" "No it wasn't me … it was you!"* It's always something silly. So what's the big deal about taking wrong on one of those? Nine times out of ten the natural process of time bears out that you weren't wrong. For example: my wife says we're supposed to go to light and turn right. I know we're supposed to turn left, but, I'm going to take wrong and say, *"Okay."* We turn right and three to five minutes later she's saying, *"This doesn't look familiar."* It becomes obvious that I was right and she was wrong and I didn't have to say anything. Get used to taking wrong. It will pay off in the long run I assure you.

- *"The fool vents all of his feelings but a wise man holds them back." (Proverbs 29:11)*

Wow! The word *fool* is kind of harsh and I wouldn't want to call anybody a fool, so let's rephrase it this way; *"The emotionally immature vents all his feelings, but a man (or woman) with emotional maturity holds them back."* There is a lot of wisdom in watching what you say.

Jesus himself gives a compelling argument for emotional maturity in Matthew 12:36. He says, *"But I say to you that for every idle word men may speak, they will give an account of it in the Day of Judgment, for by your words you will be justified and by your words you will be condemned."*

How serious is that! You will give an account for <u>every word</u> on the Day of Judgment! It's so easy to spew venomous and poisonous words at your spouse now but <u>you are going to be held accountable for every one of those words in the Day of Judgment</u>! That puts a lot of weight, a lot of importance on your ability to keep that switch in the *On* position and be emotionally mature.

In the first three chapters of this book you've been given several principles and techniques such as…

- The Hierarchy of Priorities
- The Importance of Hearing from God

- The Three Levels of Communication
- The L.I.V.E. Technique, and…
- Understanding and Expressing Anger.

These are tools that have been put in your tool box. The question is; **are you applying them to your marriage?**

As I mentioned in the Introduction, this book is part of an intense twelve-week group program called **The Marriage Miracle**. The information in this chapter is covered in week four of the program. And I have found that at this point in week four, it is common to discover that some of the couples in the group are not actually using the techniques taught up to this point.

I'll hear a couple talking about a disagreement they had that week, and I will ask, *"Did you get to the root of anger and find out what the block goal was?"*

Answer: *"No we didn't do that…"*

"Did the two of you sit down and use the L.I.V.E. Technique to talk through it?"

Answer: *"No, we were too angry and she just walked off."*

From this I can clearly see the importance of this lesson on emotional maturity.

<u>In order for these principles and techniques to work in your marriage, both you and your spouse must have the emotional maturity to apply them.</u>

In Mark chapter 4 Jesus gives a parable that has become known as The Parable of Soils. It says that *"the sower sows the seed"* which He later tells His disciples is the Word, *"and some of it falls on the wayside, some of it falls on the stony ground, some upon the thorny ground, and some on good soil."*

The four types of soils in this parable can be related to the four types of readers of this book:

The Wayside: Concerning the seed that falls on the wayside, He says that the enemy comes in and snatches it up quickly and doesn't even allow it time to take root.

I would equate that to those of you who read every chapter but by the time you put this book down, the enemy quickly distracts you and steals what you've learned. Because you can't remember what you read, you cannot apply it. Because you cannot apply it – your circumstances never change.

The Stony Ground: Of the stony ground, Jesus says there's a little bit of dirt on the stones so the seed takes root and springs up fast, but because there is no depth of earth, no nourishment for the root and the sprout, when the noon sun comes out it can't take the heat and it dries up and dies.

I would equate that to those of you who, after reading just the first few chapters are saying, *"We're good ... this book is awesome and we're all better!"*

That may sound wonderful in the moment, but when the troubles of life hit your marriage (i.e., the noon sun), it's very likely that your marriage will dry up and die because your actions were not rooted in deep understanding of each principle.

The Thorny Ground: The thorny ground is very interesting to me because the soil seems to be good and the seed takes root and actually begins to grow, but the cares of life (i.e., the thorns) grow up and begin to choke out the plant and kill it.

I would equate that to those of you who are actually taking the principles in this book, applying them to your marriage, the seed has taken root and it's beginning to grow, but all of your extenuating circumstances are cropping up and choking the life out of the fruit that has been produced. Those thorns can be all kinds of things; blended family issues, extended family issues, job issues, and the list goes on.

The Good Soil: And then there is the fourth soil and that is the good soil that Jesus said will receive the seed, allow the roots to go down deep for nourishment, and will produce a plant that in turn reproduces good fruit. Jesus goes on to say that no one can predict how much fruit this plant will produce;

"Some thirty, some sixty, some a hundred fold." But it is very clear: this is healthy soil that produces a healthy plant.

I would equate that to those of you who are applying the principles of this book deep into your minds and your understanding. You're taking each lesson very seriously and being emotionally mature to apply them to your marriage. In time, you will see the fruit—your circumstances will slowly but surely change from unhealthy to healthy. And if that were not good enough, eventually, you will share what you've learned and experienced with other couples who think that there is no hope for their marriage and see God save their marriages just like He saved yours! Some of you thirty, some of you sixty, and some of you a hundred fold!

Now if you thought you were predestined to be one of those categories of soil, it could be very depressing. You might say, *"Well, our marriage is the thorny ground, so there is no hope for us … the cares of life are going to choke it out."* **I don't believe that.** I actually believe that you get to choose which kind of ground you are and if you see in your circumstances that you are the thorny soil, or the stony ground, or the wayside – you have the ability to choose to become the good soil; to actually take these principles and apply them. They are seeds of truth, and when you receive them, and apply them to your marriage, **they will produce life and health**!

So the question again is:

Are you going to have the emotional maturity to apply them?

The couples that do well in **The Marriage Miracle** program and the ones who read this book are the ones that have the emotional maturity to lay down their selfishness and apply what they have learned. So, I want to give you two challenges for this week:

The first is to leave your emotional maturity switch in the *On* position when interacting with your spouse, refuse to reach down like a ten year old and flip it *Off*—leave your emotional maturity switch *On*.

And the second is to have the emotional maturity to <u>work on yourself</u> and allow your spouse to work on himself or herself.

Chapter Five

How to Have a Healthy Disagreement

One of the first things to understand about disagreements is what causes them in the first place. If you understand the word *precipitation*, you know that precipitation causes rain: the ocean's water vapors go up and fill the clouds, the wind carries the clouds over to land, and the temperature of the air over land at some point causes the clouds to drop the water and we call that rain. So when there is precipitation, you can bet your bottom dollar at some point along the way there is going to be rain. Disagreements work very much the same way. And by the way, it's not a matter of IF you have disagreements in a marriage; it's a matter of WHEN—because they ARE going to happen! It's actually pretty unrealistic to think that you're going to live without disagreements because they are going to happen. So what precipitates a disagreement—what causes them to happen?

Disagreements arise when:

- We cannot control a situation.
- Our rights are threatened.
- Our self-esteem is threatened.
- Others do not value us.
- We fear change.

Read back over the list above and think about those for a minute. Any one of those factors is going to turn into a disagreement.

Next, it's important to understand that there are three potential outcomes to every disagreement:

- Lose/lose
- Win/lose
- Win/win

Let's look at them closely…

Lose/lose: nobody likes a *lose/lose* disagreement.

Win/lose: unfortunately there are a lot of people who are satisfied with this one as long as they're the one that's winning; *"You got to win last time, so I'm winning this one!"* and that's where a lot of couples are stuck. One spouse wants to win the disagreement so badly he or she doesn't care if the other spouse loses. This is a very unhealthy outcome to a disagreement.

Win/win: believe it or not, a *win/win* is possible every single time. I know that may be hard to believe, but it's true; a *win/win* is possible every time there is a disagreement.

Disagreement Patterns

No two people will agree on everything; **married couples are destined to have many disagreements**. As a matter of fact, if you examine your marriage you will probably find that <u>you disagree in patterns; repeating the same disagreement with a new set of circumstances</u>.

  This has been the case in just about every couple we have ever counseled. If I could be a little fly on the wall of their home and just watch them for a couple of days, I could codify their disagreement patterns. I could say, "When John does this—Suzie does that—every time!" And, "When Suzie does that, oh… John comes back like this—every time!" I could actually map out the pattern and show it to them—and probably even show them how often the cycle repeats itself. In some cases it may be three times a day, in other cases it may be once a week, but there is always a pattern and a cycle to our disagreements.

  Let me give you an example: If a husband thinks that his wife is too controlling, a disagreement may ensue when she presents him with a honey-do list that he thinks is unreasonable. On another occasion a disagreement explodes when his wife insists on eating Chinese and he's craving Mexican. It's the same disagreement with a different set of circumstances.

Think about it for a minute; in the first case, the husband wakes up on a Saturday and he thinks, *"I've got a day off, I've got some time to myself,"* until his wife hands him a long honey-do list. When he takes a look at it, he thinks, *"Great, there goes my day, I'm not going to have any fun, I'm not going to be able to do anything I wanted to do today because my control freak wife has already got my whole day planned!"* and then the disagreement begins. But the real root of his anger is that he feels his wife is too controlling.

In the next case; they're leaving church and he's craving Mexican and she says, *"We're going to go eat Chinese food"* and they have a disagreement over that. But you see <u>it's the same problem surfacing in different circumstances</u>: again, he feels like she's being too controlling.

It's common for couples to come in for counseling and say, *"We argue about everything … we argue all the time."* Well, it's probably not many different arguments—it's probably the same one or two arguments coming out in different sets of circumstances. In many cases, one spouse has a stronger personality that dominates the smaller disagreements, but even the most passive spouse will eventually jump into fight mode.

Now this I understand personally because in our relationship Evie is the stronger personality. She is a director and she wants to plan things out. Well I'm pretty detailed too, but I'm more laid back. So I would just let it build, and build because, unfortunately, I had a tendency to be passive aggressive and would simply not participate in the conversation. But she would still win, so I would just let that build up inside of me until one day it would all come out! It's like shaking up a Coke bottle and then spraying it; all the pressure comes out at one time. So, even the most passive or laid back spouse will eventually shift into fight mode.

If disagreements are inevitable—and they are—how can a couple minimize their occurrence and resolve them effectively? The first step in minimizing and resolving disagreements is <u>to head them off at the pass</u>. You say, *"Paul that sounds very simple, but I don't know if we can do that."* You can if you will follow these steps.

Once you've identified a pattern, sit down and discuss it and develop a plan to handle every subsequent occurrence. This conversation must take place when everything is good between the two of you. Do NOT do this at a time when your emotions are running high and you're upset with each other. Do this at a time when you're calm and everything is happy and good.

Just sit down together and say, *"Okay, let's try this exercise; let's take a look at our disagreements and see if we can identify the pattern and come up with a plan to head them off at the pass."* Then work through the following three steps:

1. Agree on what the disagreement looks like; its common characteristics.

In our case, I was able to quickly identify the first pattern: every time I felt like Evie was trying to control me—I would get upset and shift into passive-aggressive mode. Likewise, Evie was able to identify a second pattern: when she would ask me to get something done, I would procrastinate and that would cause her to be even more controlling!

2. Agree on how one can cue the other when the problem begins.

This doesn't have to be in an elaborate code system. For us it was very simple; Evie agreed that I would cue her by saying, *"You're doing it again, I know you don't realize it, but you're putting pressure on me."* And I agreed that Evie's cue to me would be simply asking, *"By what time will you do that?"* And I would give her the time. So we established our cues. By the way, it is important that each spouse gets to decide what cue will be used on them. For example, Evie decided that she wanted her cue from me to be, *"You're doing it again…"* This adds great safety in using them because they were prescribed by the other.

3. Agree on what will happen when the cue is given.

In our calm discussion, Evie agreed that when I gave her the cue, she would simply back off. And likewise, I agreed that when she gave me my cue, I would simply give her the day and time I would get something done. Again, it's very important that each spouse gets to decide what action they will take when being cued. This adds great safety because—in the moment—neither feels pushed or dominated by the other; you're simply following through with what you agreed to do.

If you wait until the disagreement begins—and emotions are running high—you will simply get the same terrible results you're getting now. However, you really can head disagreements off at the pass by following the above three steps.

20 Disagreement Tips

How do you have a healthy disagreement when all efforts of avoidance fail? The following 20 tips should help.

TIME OUT: if a disagreement gets to a boiling point and you realize that you cannot discuss things CALMLY and RESPECTFULLY, call for a *Time Out* and wait until you are both calm.

SILENCE: Do not refuse to talk. Remember, one of the highest forms of disrespect is refusing to respond. The *silent treatment* is rarely, if ever, productive.

SARCASM: Avoid sarcasm—it is a form of mockery; not a good strategy for disagreements.

DON'T BULLY: The stronger personality will have a tendency to push the other spouse into a corner. Realize that this is very unhealthy, unproductive, and discourages the other spouse from trying to communicate his or her feelings.

TIME & PLACE: While many disagreements are spontaneous, be mature and hold your tongues until you are in a place where you can focus on communicating effectively.

AUDIENCES: Resolve your disagreements privately. DO NOT ARGUE IN FRONT OF CHILDREN!

ATTACK: Attack the problem—not each other.

FOCUS: Focus on the issue at hand and avoid bringing up other issues just to balance the score.

VOLUME: Watch your volume. Increased volume = increased loss of control.

TONE: Be respectful. Don't speak in a condescending tone.

INTERRUPTING: Refuse the temptation to interrupt your spouse when he or she is speaking. Allow him or her ample time to complete their points.

LABELING: Avoid name calling and labeling.

MANIPULATION: Do not use tears, ultimatums, or threats to manipulate.

SCORE KEEPING: Refuse the urge to win this one because you've lost the last 3.

LISTEN: Don't think ahead to your next rebuttal. Sincerely listen to your spouse's feelings.

AFFIRM: Affirm your spouse's thoughts, feeling, and concerns; *"what I'm hearing you say is…"*

ADMIT GUILT: Do you think you're always right? Wrong: no one is always right. Take full responsibility for your words and actions. If you're wrong—admit it quickly. Apologize and express your willingness to change.

USE "I": Use the word "I" more than the word "YOU." Speak for yourself and do not put words in your spouse's mouth.

RESOLUTION: Don't put the matter off to another time; talk it through until you come to a mutually acceptable resolution.

LEARN: Learn from every disagreement—grow in wisdom—let the disagreement teach you something about your spouse; what upsets him or her—use what you've learned to break the pattern of disagreement.

Renewing Your Mind

Ephesians 4:15 encourages us to speak the truth IN LOVE and goes on to say in verse 22, *"...put off, concerning your former conduct, the old man which grows corrupt according to the deceitful lusts, 23 and be renewed in the spirit of your mind, 24 and that you put on the new man which was created according to God, in true righteousness and holiness. 25 Therefore, putting away lying, "Let each one of you speak truth with his neighbor," for we are members of one another. 26 "Be angry, and do not sin": do not let the sun go down on your wrath, 27 nor give place to the devil."*

So, be renewed in the spirit of your mind; let these biblically based techniques wash your mind by replacing the old techniques. Put off your former conduct—the way that you used to handle disagreements—and take on this new mind. These new principles that are founded in Godly wisdom will slowly become your new habits—your new way of handling disagreements that lead to a *win/win* solution every time.

Chapter Six

The Importance of Forgiveness

Pick anyone of the seven billion people living on planet earth to live with and that person would eventually hurt you. So the opportunity to forgive is not *if*, it's *when*. Every married person will eventually be hurt by his or her spouse; it's just going to happen. As a matter of fact I think sometimes one of our biggest mistakes is to buy into the idea that marriage is going to be perfect. THERE ARE NO PERFECT MARRIAGES. I've counseled hundreds and hundreds of couples over decades and I have yet to find a perfect marriage. <u>Every married person will eventually face the challenge to forgive</u>.

So I've got a question for you: What are some circumstances in which a spouse should <u>not</u> forgive? Think about that for a minute. The answer is: there are none. There are no circumstances in which a spouse should withhold his or her forgiveness.

I've posed this question to hundreds of couples and the answer is the same every time; <u>there are no circumstances in which a spouse should withhold forgiveness</u>. Isn't that interesting? We think it through logically and come up with that answer, but in the heat of the moment, we're not so quick to come to that conclusion.

When a person has a difficult time forgiving his or her spouse, what is really going on deep down inside?

There are seven possible answers and I would like to share them one by one with you. (I'll use a wife in these examples, although it could be either wife or husband.)

1. The wife hurts badly and wants her spouse to feel and understand just how badly she hurts. It's as though she is saying; *"I want you to know how badly I'm hurting, so I'm going to withhold my forgiveness."* Or possibly, *"I can't forgive you for that because I want you to hurt—just like you hurt me."* That could be the reason.

2. She feels as though forgiveness would be condoning the offense—like giving a free pass and saying, *"What you did was really not that big of a deal."* So instead, by withholding forgiveness, she infers, *"I want to make it clear to you that I don't condone what you just did—it was wrong!"* That is another possibility.

3. Her goal of being married to someone who would never do such a thing has just been blocked. Do you remember our previous lesson on anger? (The root of anger is a blocked goal—and the person or thing that

blocked my goal is the target of my anger.) So in this case, she may be using unforgiveness to strike back.

4. She may be using her unforgiveness to set boundaries, in other words saying, *"I'll never allow you to do that to me again!"* This is actually pretty common. She's not even processing these thoughts consciously, but subconsciously—by withholding her forgiveness—she feels like she's setting boundaries.

I'd like to make a note here concerning boundaries. There are many cases where boundaries should be set, but they should be set in a healthy way and not by withholding forgiveness. For example: a wife who is being physically abused by her husband. (Remember: we decided just a few paragraphs back that there are no circumstances in which a spouse should refuse to forgive.) A good way for her to set healthy boundaries would be to tell her husband, *"I forgive you, but I will not subject myself to your abuse any longer. The kids and I are going to stay with my mother while you get help with your anger. I want to do everything I can to make this marriage work—I'll even go to counseling—but I must set some healthy boundaries for myself and the kids while we're getting help."* By saying that, she forgives her husband AND sets healthy boundaries.

5. She may use her unforgiveness to punish her husband. Oh, this one is huge! *"You hurt me very badly! ... I will never—NEVER forgive you for that!"* The thinking here is that by shaming her husband, she is punishing him.

6. Holding on to a wrong doing may be a subconscious attempt to justify one's own shortcomings. Now this one is kind of complex, so let me break it down a little bit. Let's say that the wife has a secret sin in her life and she realizes that she could eventually get caught—and when she does, her husband is going to go ballistic. So when he does something wrong to her—she's going to seize the opportunity to over-emphasize his error; *"I cannot BELIEVE you did that to me!"* So when her sin surfaces, she can go back and say, *"Oh yeah, but what about you—remember what you did? I guess this just evens the score!"* So again, it's a way of hedging her bet—so to speak.

    You might be thinking, *"Paul who would be so childish as to do that?"* Well, a lot of people—because they don't have the emotional maturity in the moment to do the right thing and forgive.

7. Here's the last one, and this one is equally complex and difficult to understand; it is <u>holding on to a wish that the past could have been different</u>. Now this is a tough one, if you think about it; who would hold on to a wish

like that when they know they can't go back and change the past? The answer is: a wife that is so sick over what her husband did to her; as long as she is holding on to that unforgiveness, there is a possibility that one day she's going to wake up and realize the whole thing was just a dream. But as soon as she forgives him—it solidifies in her mind that it really DID happen.

Those are some of the underlying reasons why spouses withhold forgiveness. Did you see yourself in any of those examples? I believe we all could if we were totally honest.

So here is another question for you: What are some of the benefits of withholding forgiveness? Are there any benefits at all? Well this question is like the one I asked before and the answer is the same; No, there are none. It is very important that you let that sink down into your mind: <u>Withholding forgiveness produces no benefits whatsoever</u>. However, it does produce many negative side effects, and here are just some of them: The unforgiven spouse…

1. feels hopeless, and you know the Bible says that, *"Hope deferred makes the heart sick."(Proverbs 13:12)*

2. becomes frustrated—feeling as if he or she has been given a life sentence.

3. has little incentive to forgive when the tables are turned.

4. begins to feel less loved.

At this point, it would be good to clarify what forgiveness *is* and what forgiveness *is not*. I'll start with a list of things that forgiveness *is not*. Forgiveness is not…

1. Simple remorse—as in, *"I'll feel bad if I don't forgive you."*

2. Forgetting—this is probably the most popular misconception of forgiveness—I hear it all the time; *"I can't forgive because I can't forget."* But <u>forgiving and forgetting are two different things</u>. You will never completely forget what happened, but you can certainly forgive.

3. Excusing or pardoning—in other words, it's not a *get out of jail free* card.

4. Trusting—this is another big misconception; <u>forgiveness and trust are two different things</u>; forgiveness is granted—trust must be earned.

5. Just a feeling—you don't just forgive when you feel like it. Actually, in most cases you're NOT going to feel like forgiving.

Now I want to give you a list of several things that forgiveness *is*. Forgiveness is…

1. Surrendering your right to judge. In other words, you're saying, *"Who am I to judge? Let God judge him."*

2. A release of all indebtedness—*"You don't owe me anything; not even another explanation."*

3. A choice to obey—*"I'm going to forgive by faith because I know it's what my Heavenly Father has instructed me to do."*

4. A gift of grace. We cannot forgive on our own, only Jesus can accomplish forgiveness. Think about that; it takes the Holy Spirit in us to forgive.

5. A freeing experience offered to the offender. Now we don't have to go very far for an example for this one. Just think of the last time that somebody forgave you—you know that feeling of freedom—and it feels awesome!

6. A precondition to love. Wow, that's a heavy one! So does that mean that I can't truly love unless I'm able to forgive someone? Yes; if you really love someone, you will forgive them. (Not to mention Jesus' admonishment to *"Love those who despitefully use you."*)

7. God's answer to anger.

Consider the words of Ephesians chapter 4, verse 29, *"Let no corrupt word proceed out of your mouth, but what is good for necessary edification, that it may impart grace to the hearers, and do not grieve the Holy Spirit of God by whom you were sealed for the day of redemption. Let all bitterness, wrath, anger, clamor, and evil speaking be put away from you with all malice, be kind one to another, tender hearted,* **forgiving one another even as God in Christ forgave you.***"* What a powerful statement!

I also want to quote Colossians 3:12, it says, *"Therefore as the elect of God, which is us, holy and beloved, put on tender mercies, kindness, humility, meekness, longsuffering, bearing with one another and forgiving one another. If anyone has a complaint against another,* **even as Christ forgave you, so you also must do***."*

So that, that brings us to the next question: Why should you forgive? There are several answers that may apply…

1. *"Because you were forgiven."* God forgave me and I didn't deserve it. As a matter of fact, if He didn't forgive you, your future would have been eternity in hell! Think about that. Did you deserve the forgiveness that God gave you? Absolutely not! Did you deserve the price that Jesus paid to take your sins upon Himself so that you could be forgiven? Absolutely not! <u>You should forgive because you were forgiven</u>!

2. *To free up fellowship with Jesus.* Now that one sounds kind of religious I suppose unless you dig down and think about it. It's tough to have communication with Jesus with that glaring unforgiveness in your heart. If you were to be completely honest, you'd probably say that every time you start praying—that thing comes to your mind, and it becomes a block between you and your communication with Christ.

3. *To free yourself with others.* When you're harboring unforgiveness against someone, especially your spouse, there is tension between the two of you and that tension discourages interaction. <u>Forgiveness restores healthy communication</u>.

4. *Because God will forgive you the same way that you forgive others.* Now this point is HUGE! Let's take a look at Matthew 6:14—and I want to preface it by saying this: These words were the words of Jesus, Emmanuel, God with us—so this is God in the flesh speaking to us. Many people might say, *"I wish I could get a word from God on this."* Well, this is as clear a word from God as you can get; this is God speaking through His Son Jesus directly to us. He says:

> *"For if you forgive men their trespasses your heavenly Father will also forgive you, but if you do not forgive*

men their trespasses neither will your Father forgive you your trespasses." (Matthew 6:14)

That is powerful and heavy! If you forgive—God is going to forgive you. If you don't forgive—God is NOT going to forgive you. We have a tendency to think that God is so loving and kind—and, of course He is, but there is justice in love. You forget that part and think, *"He loves me so much that He's going to forgive me even though I have not forgiven my spouse."* Not based on this scripture.

Consider this; the next time you are faced with giving or withholding forgiveness, imagine the Holy Spirit saying to you; *"By your actions, you are about to show God how you want Him to forgive you."* And then make your decision. That changes everything!

Forgiveness requires that you, first of all, change your behavior. Remember; forgiveness is not a feeling—it is a conscious choice. So you must change your behavior. Never use the past against your spouse. That is so tough to do—especially two months later when you're in an argument and you're losing, and you're grabbing for ammo; you'll want to reach back to the past and pull up an offense—but refuse to do it! <u>Never use the past against your spouse again</u>.

Remember when I said that forgiving and forgetting are two different things? Here is a saying that I would encourage you to memorize…

If remembered—then remember that it was forgiven.

Every time the thought of that person hurting you comes to mind, the thought that should come in right behind it is, *"Yes … and I remember I forgave that person too, that's a done deal."*

Changing Your Mindset

The next thing you've got to do is make a conscious decision to <u>change your mindset and think feel good thoughts about your spouse</u>. If you dwell on the offense it can begin to eat your lunch. The longer you dwell on a thought the more it becomes a feeling, and that feeling will lead to an action. The next thing you know, you've said or done something that you will regret.

Ask God to help you. I often quote James 1:5, *"If any of you lacks wisdom, let him ask of God, who gives to all liberally and without reproach, and it will be given to him."* So if you need help with this, ask God to help you to forgive and acknowledge that your spouse has the ability to change.

I know all of the old sayings; *A leopard can't change his spots*, and, *Once a cheater—always a cheater*. Those are what I call *cultural lies*. If they were true, then we're all doomed to hell for eternity because you heard that *Once a sinner—always a sinner!* No! That's not true—and there is nothing in the Bible that supports that thought. As a matter of fact, there is a ton of evidence in the Bible that says EXACTLY THE OPPOSITE! So, again, acknowledge the fact that your spouse has the ability to change.

Forgiveness can be learned and become a part of your everyday life. When we walk in forgiveness, we walk in total love. God is love, and when we forgive we are allowing God's love to flow through us to our spouse.

How do you want God to forgive you—partially or completely? Answer that question and forgive your spouse the same way.

Chapter Seven

When Selfishness Connects With Authority

What happens when selfishness connects with authority? I want to start by reading Ephesians chapter 5, verses 22 through 30. *"Wives submit to your own husbands as to the Lord for the husband is head of the wife, as also Christ is head of the church and He is the Savior of the body; therefore just as the church is subject to Christ so let the wives be to their own husbands in everything. Husbands love your wives, just as Christ also loved the church and gave Himself for her that He might sanctify and cleanse her with the washing of water by the Word that He might present her to Himself a glorious church not having spot or wrinkle or any such thing, but that she should be holy and without blemish. So husbands ought to love their own wives as their own bodies, he who loves his wife loves himself, for no one ever hated his own flesh but nourishes and cherishes it just as the Lord does the church, so we are members of His body, of His flesh and of His bones."*

Now this is an incredible metaphor that Paul is creating, drawing a parallel between the husband/wife relationship and the relationship Christ has with His bride the church. That is what God wants every marriage to look like. Unfortunately, the enemy has declared war on marriages.

Divide and Conquer, that is the strategy of the enemy when it comes to marriages. If he can simply get you on opposite sides of the battlefield, he doesn't need to defeat you, you will defeat yourselves. Isn't that true? He just has to cause opposition and get you to start shooting at each other and then he can back out of the battle. He doesn't have to do any more work; you will finish yourselves off. Interestingly enough, the enemy uses a relatively short list of common problems to initiate your self-destruction.

Years ago I decided to do a little study on what causes marriage problems. I expected to come up with a very long list of marriage killers, but I was surprised to find out how short the list really was. Things like…

- Poor communication
- Abuse
- Financial conflicts
- Lust
- Pride

I'm not saying that that list sums up every marriage problem, but I've counseled a lot of people and most of the time it fits into one of those categories. When I ask, *"What do you guys argue about?"* They say, *"We argue about everything; you name it—*

we argue about it! We have all kinds of problems!" The truth is, you probably don't have a lot of different problems; you probably have a few problems that surface in different ways in different circumstances.

That short list can actually be reduced to one single common denominator: SELFISHNESS. Every device used to destroy marriages and families is rooted in selfishness.

Take a good look at the problems in your marriage and in your home; every single one of them is rooted in selfishness. Just think back to the last problem you and your spouse had—selfishness was in there somewhere. **Selfishness is at the root of every marital problem.** Selfishness is one of the greatest weaknesses of man. It is a very, very powerful force and every single one of us has a measure of selfishness.

There is another very powerful force and that is the force of AUTHORITY. Spiritual authority is an amazing thing; it really is. God who is all powerful and the ultimate authority of the universe chose to delegate to every man and woman a measure of authority. When God delegates that authority He never usurps it, which means He never takes it back or works around it to manipulate you to do something. Once He delegates that authority—it's final. He doesn't say, *"You're not doing a good job using the authority I gave you, so I'm going to take it back from you."* He doesn't take it back. He delegates it and He refuses to violate our will to make us do something. So it's up to you how you use your authority.

God gives you authority over many things in your life and the lives of others. Even with all of His power, God refuses to usurp the authority He has delegated—<u>even when someone abuses it</u>. Now *that* blows me away!

It is in His sovereignty that He chooses to do it this way. But sometimes I think that if I was God, and I delegated a man the authority to be a father—and I saw him about to abuse his son, I would probably reach down and grab his fist and say; *"Oh no you're not gonna do that ... that's my boy you're about to hit."* I'm admitting that I don't understand it all, but I do know that in His sovereignty, God does not do that; once He gives that man the authority to be that little boy's father—it's a done deal and that father can either choose to use his authority properly or abuse it—and God will not change that.

Everyone wants authority. It's not uncommon at all—people like having authority.

But what you sometimes fail to realize is that <u>with authority comes responsibility</u>; they're attached at the hip. You can't have one and not have the other:

Husbands have authority, but they also have the *responsibility* to love their wives just like Christ loves His bride, the church.

Wives have authority, but they also have the *responsibility* to submit to their husband's even as unto the Lord.

Parents have authority, but they also have the *responsibility* to raise their children in the nurture and admonition of Christ.

Even children have a measure of authority, but they also have the *responsibility* to obey their parents for this is right in God.

Authority is a very, very powerful force, and <u>every one has a measure of authority</u>.

So you have the force of SELFISHNESS and you have the force of AUTHORITY. Here is another significant principle that you would do well to memorize…

When SELFISHNESS connects with AUTHORITY… BAD THINGS HAPPEN!

Like fire and gunpowder, when these two connect—bad things happen. When a husband allows selfishness to connect with his authority to speak to his wife—bad things happen. A husband may get all 'big and bad' thinking, *"I'm the man of this house, I'm the head of my wife, I'm angry, so I'm gonna say whatever I want! I'm gonna start calling her names, I'm gonna start tearing her down, and I'm gonna abuse her emotionally if I see fit!"* That's what happens when selfishness connects with his authority.

When a wife allows selfishness to connect with her authority to seek affection from someone other than her husband—bad things happen. A woman may say, *"Hey, I'm not getting the affection I deserve from my husband, I'm grown, I'm my own woman, so if I want to chat with this guy online—that's up to me!"* She's allowed selfishness to connect with her authority and—bad things happen.

When a parent allows selfishness to connect with his authority to discipline his children—bad things happen. (Oh this is rampant!) His child comes home with an "F" on his report card and he says, *"Oh boy you are going to get it! You don't come into this house with an "F," you're gonna get the beatin' of your life boy!"* Is an "F" a problem? Yes. Is there a need for some type of discipline? Probably. But all the bullying rhetoric is a parent who's allowed selfishness to connect with his/her authority and --bad things happen. (If you like, take a moment and see if you can theorize the root of this father's anger.)

When you allow selfishness to connect with your authority—bad things happen and marriages begin to fall apart. You probably don't have to look very far to see this principle at work in your home.

So let's take another look at Ephesians chapter 5, verse 22. It says, *"Wives submit to your own husbands as to the Lord."* And verse 25 says, *"Husbands love your wives just as Christ also loved the church."* These scriptures are often quoted by husbands and wives. The problem is they are usually quoted with a selfish bent. It goes something like this; a husband says to his wife, *"You HAVE to submit to me … it's commanded of you right here in the Bible!"* He's actually using the Bible as a bully pulpit; *"It's right here in black and white; God said it and you have to submit to me!"* Or, the wife may say to her husband, *"You are supposed to love me just like Christ loved the church, so you HAVE to be good to me!"* They are using the scriptures to make their point, but I'm sure you can see the selfishness in those statements. You take the Word and use it to your advantage in your arguments, but the motive is selfishness.

So I've got a question for you; what if Christ loved you like you love each other? He would say things like, *"I don't like what you said to me, so I'm not talking to you anymore!"* Or He might say, *"When you start respecting me, I'll start respecting you!"* Or how about this one, *"You don't fulfill my needs anymore; so I want you out of my life!"* Is that how you want Christ to respond to you? Absolutely not, but you are quick to do it with your spouse.

Why does Christ not respond to you that way? Because...

Jesus does not connect selfishness with His authority... and neither should you!

What happens when you connect selfishness with authority? Say it with me... BAD THINGS HAPPEN!

Ephesians chapter 5, verses 22 through 30, are actually some of the most unselfish scriptures in the entire Bible. They are not driven by selfishness; they are driven by self-less-ness; *"I'm putting you above myself."* Jesus puts you above Himself. He gave His own life so that you and I wouldn't have to suffer damnation. He laid down His life for you, and you should do the same when it comes to your spouse. That is the spirit of Ephesians chapter 5.

<u>Understanding these scriptures will revolutionize your concept of a Christian marriage.</u>

- So take selfishness out of your disagreements.
- Take selfishness out of your decisions.
- Take selfishness out of your discipline for your children
- Take selfishness out of your authority...

...and you will see the problems that are tearing your marriage apart leave your home—one by one.

Unselfish love will strengthen a marriage.

Unselfish love will build a happy home.

Unselfish Christ-like love will make a marriage whole.

Chapter Eight

Breaking the Vicious Argument Cycle
(Husband's Role as Leader)

In the previous chapter we covered the topic When Selfishness Connects with Authority and there is no doubt that each spouse has a level of authority in a marriage. But the struggle for authority often leads to a vicious cycle of arguing and this cycle can last for years unless both spouses identify it and take deliberate steps to end it.

Let's start by dissecting the argument cycle and analyzing each part.

There are four main ingredients:

1. Offensive Words: A statement produced from anger, disappointment or frustration.
2. Fears: things that a person does not want to experience.
3. Reactions: Verbal and non-verbal responses.
4. Counter-Attacks: An attempt to overcome the offense and strike back.

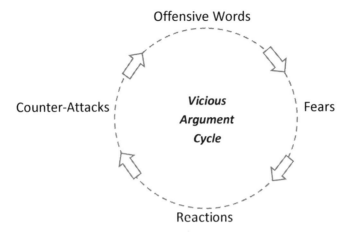

Offensive Words: As you can see in the chart above, the impetus of an argument is the initial offensive word spoken by a spouse. It is important to understand that the words may or may not be intentionally offensive. As a matter of fact they are often not intentionally offensive, but they can be perceived that way because you hear through the filter of perceived reality.

Offensive words are a statement produced from anger, disappointment or frustration. That first offensive word strikes some type of fear inside of the other spouse.

Fears: By *fear* I don't mean something that you're scared of like falling out of a 20-story building. I mean *"fear"* as in something that you don't want to feel or experience. You could consider this fear a raw nerve deep down inside the person, possibly an emotional wound from the past. When that raw nerve is struck by offensive words it causes an instant, often uncontrollable reaction. The reactions can be verbal and non-verbal responses, and by the way, non-verbal responses can be just as bad as the verbal responses; the look on your face or the fact that you just clam up and walk out of the room. The reactions lead very naturally into a counter attack.

Counter Attacks: The counter attack is an attempt to overcome the offense and strike back—which causes there to be more offensive words that hit more fears, which cause more reactions and so on, and this vicious cycle begins to spin out of control.

So let me break down the cycle for you: The cycle usually begins with an offensive word that, at its core, strikes an area of fear in the other spouse. Note the phrase *at its core*. Again, it might not be something spoken with the intention of being offensive or upsetting, but at its core there is something there that strikes a fear in the other spouse. The statement may, and usually does, have an underlying message that is more impactful than the actual words spoken. A statement such as, *"I guess I'll just do these dishes myself"* may be interpreted as, *"You are lazy, you never help around the house, and I am forever cleaning up after you!"* The offended spouse then reacts in a very defensive manner and then launches a counter attack thus spinning the cycle into its next turn.

List of Common Fears

So what are these fears? The following is a list of common emotional fears.

1. Failure: A fear of failure might be for a man to think that, because there is a cancellation notice for the electricity in the mailbox, he is a failure as a provider.

2. Unloved: This could come from someone who felt unloved as a child; it's a very familiar feeling to her; she can't quite put her finger on it, but something about what you just said gives her the same feeling she felt when she was young and unloved.

3. Unwanted: If someone was abandoned in some way in the past, he may interpret certain words as indications that you too will abandon him.

4. Judged: A person that has been judged by others for many years may hear your words as being very judgmental.

5. Insecurity: This one I can relate to in a big way; I've spent 30 years of my life trying to overcome insecurities. So when Evie would ask me a simple question like, *"Why did you put that there?"* — which would be a very simple question to six and a half billion other people on the planet—and the answer would be, *"Because that's where it goes."* Bbut if she asked me that same question, I would respond with something sarcastic like, *"Well what do you think—I'm an idiot for putting it there?"* Did she mean it offensively? Probably not. Did I take it offensively? Yes!

6. Powerless: A person who has been suppressed and controlled for many years may feel powerless when words are used that resemble dominance.

7. Invalidated: A person raised by a parent that never took them seriously might easily feel invalidated by words or actions similar to that of his or her parent.

8. Ineffective: If a person's efforts to make his or her spouse happy seem to go unrewarded, that person may feel ineffective, especially if they've experienced similar failures in the past.

9. Disregarded: A person who has been disregarded in the past may be especially sensitive to words or actions that they interpret as disregarding their feelings.

10. Rejection: This one is very much like insecurities; maybe a person was rejected when they were young and something about the words you're using makes him feel rejected.

11. Inadequate: This is the fear that says, *"I'm not good* *enough"* and it is often coupled with another fear such as insecurity.

List of Common Reactions

Next, I want to give you a list of reactions. These are the knee-jerk responses a person gives when one of his fears (i.e., raw nerves) are struck by words he deems offensive:

1. Anger/Rage: Harsh words, strong body language, possibly violent acts.

2. Criticize: Often an attempt to even the score or suppress the other person's opinion.

3. Sarcasm: Often stems from insecurities; it is an attempt to make the other person look smaller. I, personally, have a bent toward sarcasm. I learned sarcasm in humor, but unfortunately I also learned how to use it in my arguments.

4. Humiliate: Now this is a very childish tactic but unfortunately many adults use it. Humiliation is a quick attempt to make me look *better* by making you look *worse*.

5. Provoke: Striking one of your fears in an attempt to

draw a fight out of you or simply getting you to do or say something wrong that can be turned around and use against you.

6. Ignore: Acting as though you are not worth the breath to respond. It is an act of passive aggression in which the offender feels as though he or she is gaining power.

7. Belittle: This one is very much like humiliation but less severe. It is an attempt to minimize what another person feels or says in order to elevate ones importance.

8. Avoidance: Similar to ignore, but avoidance attempts to bypass confrontation all together.

9. Lecture: The favorite of many! *"You're going to tell me about me? Well, not only am I going to hit you on the same subject, I'm gonna bring in everything wrong you have ever done to me, and I'm gonna show you that I'm not so bad when you take a look at yourself!"* It is often a release of pent-up grievances.

10. Withdraw: Similar to avoidance and ignoring, but communicates, *"I'm going to withdraw myself from you completely. For the rest of the day you're probably not even going to know I'm in the house—and when we go to bed tonight, there is going to be an invisible line down the middle of that bed and you can rest assured I'm not going to even so* *much as bump into you with my toe!"*

11. Exaggerate: Usually used when there is not enough actual evidence to make the point. Also, common with a person who feels his/her word is not enough—he/she feel that he/she must ramp-up the facts.

12. Blame: Commonly known as *The Blame Game.* The person refuses to take responsibility for his or her actions and diverts the attention to someone else. Even if the offender admits guilt, he or she will often blame his or her actions on someone else's greater wrong doing.

Take a look at the List of Common Fears and the List of Common Reactions and you will probably find your personal combination. Mine would be: when my fear of insecurity is struck, I react with sarcasm.

Take another look and you will probably find yours and your spouse's method of Counter Attack. You know your spouse better than anyone—his or her weaknesses and vulnerabilities—and you know how to take him or her down better than anyone.

Your counter attack causes the cycle to spin into its next round and it escalates every time it goes around—it goes up a step higher and continues until either one or both of you separate in despair.

My guess is, each and every one of you has experienced The Vicious Argument Cycle in one form or another. The cycle gets started turning and it can go on for days and weeks and possibly even months. The sad part is that it is totally unproductive and it can tear a marriage apart.

Breaking the Cycle

Placing blame on who started the Vicious Argument Cycle is equivalent to the old question; *Which came first—the chicken or the egg?* The husband may say, *"What you said was very disrespectful to me"* To which the wife responds, *"I only said that because of the way you treated me yesterday morning!"* To which the husband responds, *"I only treated you that way because of what you did the night before!"* Give them long enough and they could run the blame all the way back to Adam and Eve!

So this analogy begs the question: **"Who leads the way in breaking the vicious argument cycle?"** Well, there is an answer to that question and the Bible makes it very clear; the husband leads the way. Now that may have some husbands upset with me, but remember we started this book by saying that it is based on principles of truth. You want the truth, and the only absolute for truth that I know is God's Word and I believe this is a truth that is in God's Word.

Most husbands believe that they are the head of their wife. I've never had a husband say that he didn't believe that. They also believe that they are the leader of their home; they have no problem with that either. Husbands are quick to agree to that, but that begs the next question; ***"In what are you leading?"*** Leading as defined in the Bible does not mean establishing a dictatorship, and unfortunately, that's what a lot of guys learned from their dads; *"I'm the king of this castle, what I say goes, when I say jump you say how high!"* It means <u>leading in Christ like behavior</u>; modeling Christ like characteristics before your wife and your children on a daily basis.

So let's take a another look at Ephesians chapter 5 and verse 23, it says *"For the husband is head of the wife as also Christ is head of the church and He is the savior of the body, therefore just as the church is subject to Christ, so let the wives be to their own husbands in everything. Husbands love your wives just as Christ also loved the church and gave Himself for her, that He might sanctify and cleanse her with the washing of water by the Word, that He might present her to Himself a glorious church, not having spot or wrinkle or any such thing, but that she should be holy and without blemish."*

Question: Who washes the bride? Answer: Jesus—the husband in this metaphor. He doesn't say to her, *"Woman, go clean yourself up, and when you're spotless, come back and present yourself to me."* No, He takes it upon Himself to wash her of every spot and wrinkle. This text makes it very clear that the husband leads the way in breaking The Vicious Argument Cycle by *washing* his wife with the *water* of his words and cleansing her of every spot and wrinkle, or you could say, every *fear* (i.e., her wounds). Jesus is the one that led the way by showing you that you can trust Him, that you can respect Him, that you can follow Him, and that He's always going to have your best interest at heart. The Apostle Paul gave this great metaphor, this picture of Christ as our example, and I just can't see it any other way than scripture indicating that the husband should be the one who leads the way.

This does not let the wife off the hook, by the way. If you read on to Ephesians 5:33 it says, *"Nevertheless let each one of you in particular so love his own wife as himself and let the wife see that she respects her husband."* This makes it very clear that the wife must quickly take the next step. So it is the husband who breaks The Vicious Argument Cycle by leading the way and modeling Christ like behavior and it is the wife that follows quickly in step by responding to his leadership.

Nine Fruits of the Spirit

So how does a husband begin to lead in Christ like behavior? He begins to model the nine fruits of the Spirit. These are things that you have probably heard since you were a child; however, it's my guess that most cannot quote them. So it is going to be very important for you husbands to memorize the nine fruits of the Spirit and get them deep into your spirit. Here they are:

1. Love	4. Patience	7. Faithfulness
2. Joy	5. Kindness	8. Gentleness
3. Peace	6. Goodness	9. Self-control

I listed them in pairs of three for two reasons; one is because I think it's easiest to learn them three at a time, there's a certain cadence to them in three's. The other reason is because I have found that the last three are the toughest for men: faithfulness, gentleness and self-control. Faithfulness is difficult for some husbands because they think what is done in secret doesn't really matter. Gentleness is a tough one because we are 'the man of the house;' we have a tendency to go into our authoritative mode, and it's tough to remember that we should model gentleness in front of our wife and children. Self-control goes right along with it; sometimes we just get hot and fly off the handle and say things that we don't even mean.

I encourage every husband to memorize the nine fruits of the Spirit and check yourselves daily to see that you are modeling these Christ-like behaviors in front of your wife and children. One great way to memorize them is to write them on 3x5 cards and put them up in places where you will see them regularly such as the bathroom mirror and the dashboard of your car. But whatever it takes for you, do it, and memorize the nine fruits of the Spirit and check yourself on all nine on a daily basis. Start with the first one, Love, and ask yourself; *"Am I modeling love in front of my wife and children?"* and so on throughout the entire list—every day. This is a great exercise for husbands and wives, but I want to especially encourage husbands to do this.

Men, your children, especially your sons, are learning self-control by your daily behavior. If you have a son that does not have self-control, I hate to say it, but he probably learned it from you. He picked up that behavior from you because he sees that modeled in front of him on a daily basis. But don't be discouraged; his behavior will change as yours changes.

The results of this exercise will be that your wife and children will see your Christ-like behavior and begin to willingly follow your leadership and you will break The Vicious Argument Cycle in your home once and for all.

Chapter Nine

Wife's Role as Helper

In chapter eight you learned that The Vicious Argument Cycle can be broken and that there is clear instruction in the Bible on who leads the way in breaking that cycle. Ephesians chapter 5 makes it very clear that it's the husband. Now let's shift to the wife, and take a look at her role as helper.

Leadership in any area of life can be either supported or undermined by its followers. It is important to understand that when leadership established by God is undermined serious problems will arise.

For example, when a wife becomes the predominate leader in a home, she not only inflicts undue trouble, she removes herself from the protection of her husband. This is fairly common. Couples come into our office and the wife will say, *"He will not take his rightful role as leader of our home, so I'm doing it."* Then she will go on to tell us how she is the one that calls the kids together for prayer and Bible study and she is the one that casts vision for their home and say, *"This is the direction I believe God would have us to go...,"* because her husband won't do it. That is called *usurping authority*. Usurp just means that you will take back or go around someone's authority because that person is not doing it the way you think he or she should. But when a wife usurps her husband's authority, she removes herself from his protection and leadership.

If a wife feels that her husband is not assuming leadership in any area of their marriage, she should not assume the role herself, but do everything possible to help her husband to become stronger in that area.

Here are three steps a wife can take:

1. Resist the temptation to take over. Wives, when you feel it coming on, just resist the temptation to take over, just do not succumb to it.

2. Talk to your husband and tell him your desire for him to take the lead and that you will follow his leadership when he does. Now this would be a great opportunity for you to use the L.I.V.E. Communication Technique that we learned in chapter two. Use that technique and get to the bottom of it so that you will come out with a *win/win* conclusion.

3. If nothing else works up to this point, I recommend that you consult a Christian marriage counselor to help you establish proper leadership roles in your home. I hope it doesn't take going to a counselor to do this, but

listen, if you can't resolve this one between the two of you, by all means go and see a Christian counselor. Trust God to use his or her expertise to coach you through this process and help you come up with a solution on which you both agree.

The role of wife was established by God to be a helper to her husband. Take a look at Genesis 2:18, *"And the Lord God said, It is not good that man should be alone, I will make him a helper comparable to him."* It's important to know that *helper* does not mean *servant*; it means that a wife will *complete* her husband. She will complete him by providing several things he simply can't accomplish on his own, the first of which is his counterpart for affection and sexual intimacy. Secondly, she completes her husband by providing a natural ability to nourish babies — something that comes very natural to women. The next is a feminine perspective on issues. Now this one is a big point of contention between a lot of husbands and wives. A husband will say, *"My wife has a different perspective and that frustrates me."* Well, she's supposed to have a different perspective — God made her that way! And the longer he's married the more I hope he learns to listen to his wife's perspective.

For years my wife, who has great spiritual discernment, would tell me, *"I don't feel like you should get into business with that guy."* And I would say, "What? He's a Christian and he's got a great track record!" And she would say, *"Paul I don't know what it is, but my skin crawls when he walks in the room; I just don't feel good about him."* And, oh, I would get so mad because he had the investment money I needed to make my business work!

Well guess what! She was right about 90% of the time! I can remember when I decided to start listening to her. I said, *"I'm going to start listening to her perspective and rely on it, because God has given her to me to complete me, and she sees from my blind spot—she just sees things from a perspective that I don't."* And it has served me well to this day.

And lastly, a wife provides encouragement and agreement. Now I know that doesn't come so quickly when there is contention in the marriage, but when things are working properly, a wife completes her husband by agreeing with him and encouraging him.

Three Things Husbands Hate

Together a husband and wife complete each other and become one flesh—the image of God. Because of this God-given role husbands are wired for leadership and any actions contrary to this premise will frustrate the husband.

So ladies I'm going to give you three things that husbands hate:

1. Feeling of being pushed.
2. That his wife not be burdened or tense.
3. A wife who resists him in disciplining children.

Seven Ways a Wife Destroys Her Husband's Manliness

Additionally, a wife has the ability to emasculate her husband. She's actually one of the few people on the planet who can do that to her husband. That's not so hard to understand when you know that she was created to complete her husband. If she withholds the things that complete him, it is sure to make him feel like less of a man.

The following are seven ways a wife destroys her husband's manliness:

1. Expecting him to know what you need without telling him.
2. Being financially independent.
3. Being more loyal to outside leadership than her husband.
4. Resisting his decisions in your spirit.
5. Reviewing his past failures.

6. Resisting his physical affection.

7. Taking matters into your own hands.

I'd like to clarify a few items on that list—the first of which is *#2: Being financially independent.* We've counseled many couples who maintain separate bank accounts and, truthfully, I've never seen it work very well. I know there are extreme circumstances where it may be absolutely necessary, but in most cases, it infers that the wife does not completely trust her husband to provide for her. I believe when a marriage is healthy and whole, all of the finances should be considered *ours* and not part of them *mine*.

The next is *#3: Being more loyal to outside leadership than her husband.* For example, a wife who comes home from church every Sunday saying, *"The pastor says we should do such and so,"* even though the husband has said differently. Another example of *outside leadership* might be the wife's father, or even her boss. Eventually, the husband is going to become weary of the opposing influence and blurt out something like, *"Well then why don't you go marry the pastor?"*

And finally, *#5: Reviewing his past failures.* Every husband has made mistakes and every husband wants to feel as though he is improving in life. When a wife constantly throws up his past failures, it becomes demoralizing and actually keeps him from growing.

As you can see, a wife has the ability to complete her husband and when she does, the two of them become one. Some people view scripture as preferring the husband. I see it very differently. As a matter of fact, understanding scripture the way I do now, if I had a choice, I'd prefer to be the wife! What a safe place to be; loved, cherished, provided for, secured, protected … who would not want that? It's when the enemy creeps in and persuades a husband to mistreat his wife or a wife to withhold herself from her husband that things begin to fall apart.

Washing and Healing

In chapter 8 we learned that the husband leads the way by washing his wife of every *spot* and *wrinkle* with the water of his words. One could assume that the process stops there, but I don't think so. Think about it; the simple fact that a wife is a Christian means that she exhibits Christ-like behavior—right? That being the case, she should also follow the example of Christ and begin to wash her spouse with the water of her words.

 This process of *washing* each other is very challenging because you're assuming the responsibility of cleansing your spouse of the very things that drive you crazy! In our case, Evie's negativity drove me crazy and my insecurities drove her crazy. Once we began *washing* each other with our words, I began to heal in the area of insecurities and she began to heal in the area of negativity.

As a matter of fact, I can go so far as to say this: it is YOUR responsibility to cleanse your spouse of all the things that drive you crazy about him or her.

Wife, the healing of your life's emotional wounds will come <u>through your husband</u>.

Husband, the healing of your life's emotional wounds will come <u>through your wife</u>.

I believe this is the God-ordained way for us to be healed of our emotional wounds. How clever of the enemy to distance us from the very one through whom God's healing will flow!

Evie and I once counseled a wife who was separated from her husband. Their plan was this: *"Let's separate … you work on you and I'll work on me. If and when we get ourselves fixed, we'll come back together and work on this marriage."* I can remember her saying, *"I know God can heal me from all the junk in my life that has driven my husband away from me."* Little did she know that she was distancing herself from the very one through whom God would cleans and heal her.

With the exception of extreme circumstances such as abuse, I rarely recommend separation because it is directly opposed to God's sovereign plan for marital healing. The better plan is for the husband and wife to submit themselves to an unbiased third party with a godly plan to lead them, step-by-step, to complete marital health.

Praying Effectively vs. Praying in Error

Let me go a little deeper and touch on another common problem associated with marital healing: **praying in error**. It is very common for a spouse to say, *"I've turned it all over to God and I'm claiming that our marriage is healed and this spirit of trouble will be supernaturally broken off of our marriage—in Jesus' name."* That, believe it or not, is a prayer in error. You may be thinking, *"Paul, how can you say that? That is a very sincere prayer of faith!"* No, it is a very sincere prayer in error. It's what I call hyper-faith: having more confidence in a chant of words than the actual truth of God's word.

In Jesus' Name is not a magical ending that makes a prayer come true. The prayer itself must be according to the truth of Jesus' word. To pray *In Jesus' Name* means that you are praying according to Jesus' precepts and will. And when it comes to marital healing, the *truth* is that God has ordained (to prearrange unalterably) a principle of marital healing that comes through one's spouse.

So how does one pray effectively? First, by learning exactly what God's word says about the issue: Study His principles, and then praying according to those principles. Keep this in mind: <u>God will always lead you to truth</u>. You may find the truth by studying God's word, by counseling (with someone that knows and understands God's word), or even by reading a book (based on God's word) such as this one. Here's an example of an effective prayer for marital healing; *"Father, you know my husband and I have strayed far from your plan for our marriage. I pray that You will lead us to truth and help us apply truth to our marriage. I also ask that you give me the wisdom to speak words of life to my husband and help me wash him clean by the words of my mouth. I put my trust in You and I believe that as we follow Your word—our marriage will be healed. In Jesus' name; amen."* That, my friend, is a prayer perfectly in line with Jesus' precepts and will—and one that you can believe with great faith will come to pass.

Just as The Vicious Argument Cycle spins out of control in the wrong direction, when a husband and wife begin to work together to cleanse and complete each other, the whole process begins to spin in the right direction. The end result is a healthy relationship that produces a beautiful marriage. One that neither of you would ever want to leave.

Chapter Ten

Emotional Needs

Every one of us has Emotional Needs. Dr. Willard Harley, a respected Christian psychologist, has conducted extensive studies which indicate that most adults possess a variety of ten different Emotional Needs[1]. Each of us has several at the top of our list which are called Primary Emotional Needs. The thing to understand about Primary Emotional Needs is that they are as important to our emotions as food and water are to our physical being.

Imagine a man saying, *"Since water is not easily accessible to me; I'm going to swear off water completely—I'll just do without it!"* He could say that and he could even do that, but we know where we would be thirty to sixty days later; we would be at his funeral because dehydration would overtake his internal organs and he would be physically dead.

The same thing happens with our emotions. If they are not met, we begin to starve for them and crave them. We get irritable and sometimes settle for counterfeit substitutes.

---

1. *His Needs, Her Needs: Building an Affair-Proof Marriage* by Willard F. Jr. Harley

Like a man crawling through the desert; parched and desperate for water and someone tells him, *"There's a small contaminated puddle over there"* and he would say, *"I don't care; I'll strain it through my teeth—just give it to me!"* In time, if these needs are not met, we become emotionally dead.

The following are the statistical results of Primary Emotional Needs divided by sex:

MALE	FEMALE
1. Sexual fulfillment	1. Affection
2. Admiration	2. Conversation
3. Recreational companionship	3. Honesty and openness
4. Attractiveness of spouse	4. Financial support
5. Domestic support	5. Family commitment

(It is important to understand that the two lists above are based on statistics. Your Primary Emotional Needs list may be very different.)

The most misunderstood term in the list is *Domestic support.* So allow me to clarify: domestic support does not mean getting the husband to help vacuum. It means someone to manage the home, the kids clothes, lunches, and help cook the meals, etc.

While the prioritization will vary from person to person, we all have some level of all 10 needs.

Here's a little story that will help you understand Emotional Needs:

Susie is a beautiful young lady with a great personality but no interest whatsoever in sports. Bobby is a handsome young jock who loves football. Bobby and Susie meet, are very attracted to each other, and start dating. Want to guess where they are every Monday night during football season? That's right: either in the bleachers or watching the game on television. Susie doesn't realize it, but every Monday night, she is making a deposit into Bobby's Emotional Need for recreational companionship.

Because he likes the response he gets, Bobby sends Susie flowers to her at work, gives her hugs and kisses, and says complimentary things like, *"Girl, you look so hot in that football jersey!"* Bobby doesn't realize it, but he is making regular deposits into Susie's Emotional Need for affection. When Bobby calls Susie at work, she gets excited at the very appearance of his name on her caller I.D. She answers and says, *"Hey baby! I'm not really supposed to take calls at work, but let me sneak outside for a minute so we can talk!"*

If you could hear an Emotional Need being met, you would hear a *Cha-ching!* every time Bobby and Susie make their deposits.

In time, Bobby and Susie get married and the distractions of life begin to creep in:

- The economy is bad so Susie has to take a job.
- Bobby's mother takes ill and he's at his parent's home a few nights a week taking care of her.
- Baby #1 comes along and eventually baby #2.
- Susie is offered a promotion at work, but to take it she must enroll in an evening master's program at the local college.
- Bobby is so swamped at work that when he gets home in the evening he feels as though he just left and his day was so fast-paced he didn't have a minute to order flowers for Susie.
- And on Monday nights, when Bobby's watching football, guess where Susie is; that's right; in the den on the computer studying for her final.

Because they've become distracted and are failing to make regular deposits into each other's Emotional Needs, the levels of fulfillment in those areas is getting lower … and lower … and lower until they are completely empty. And just like an empty stomach begins to growl, Bobby and Susie begin to get irritable with each other; contention settles in and arguments happen at the drop of a hat. Now, when Bobby calls Susie at work, she sees his name on her caller I.D., grimaces, and answers by saying, *"What? Can't this wait until later; I told you I'm not supposed to take calls at work!"*

One day, Susie is in the break room at work when a new male coworker comes in and says, *"That shirt really looks great on you Susie!"* (Want to say it with me? *Cha-ching!*) Susie goes back to her cubical, shakes her head and thinks, *"I don't know what just happened ... but it sure felt good!"* Before you know it, Susie is making more and more excuses to visit the break room.

> (Note: in most affairs, whether emotional or sexual, the *"Big Deal"* is not the *other person*—it's the Emotional Need that is being met by the other person.)

At this point, a couple like Bobby and Susie will end up in a marriage counselor's office saying things like,

- *"I just don't think I love him/her anymore."*
- *"The flame has flickered out."*
- *"There's just no chemistry between us anymore."*

And then they'll say something like this: *"I want it to be NATURAL like it was back then!"* But that's the lie: it wasn't NATURAL back then. It took a lot of WORK to fulfill each other's Emotional Needs. And now it's going to take a lot of WORK to make the marriage strong again.

Ivan Pavlov developed a theory of association by ringing a bell and then giving his dog a piece of meat. He repeated this process over and over until he could simply ring the bell and his dog would begin to salivate. Likewise, we humans are creatures of association. In the beginning, Susie associated warm and fuzzy feelings with Bobby to the point that the very appearance of his name on her caller I.D. gave her instant joy. When her Emotional Needs accounts became bankrupt, the same name on her caller I.D. gave Susie an instant feeling of frustration.

Here's a saying that you should memorize:

Humans avoid pain and return to pleasure.

Therefore, if you associate pain, frustration, and tension with your spouse, you will avoid him or her. On the other hand, if you associate pleasure, fun, and peace with your spouse, you will want to be with him or her.

The problem when it comes to Primary Emotional Needs is that few people know what theirs are. They can describe what they *think* is their strongest needs, but few can articulate those needs in a way that that their spouse can clearly understand them let alone know what to do to fulfill them.

It is also interesting to know that we naturally try to fulfill our spouse through the Emotional Need that is primary for us. For example, a husband may try to make his wife happy by giving her sexual fulfillment (because that is his Primary Emotional Need). Sexual fulfillment is on her list, but it's not as important to her as it is to him. Affection is her Primary

Emotional Need, but her husband never seems affectionate. Eventually, the husband is complaining to a counselor; *"I do everything I possibly can to make this woman happy, and she's never happy!"*

It is VITALLY IMPORANT that you know yours and your spouse's PRIMARY EMOTIONAL NEEDS; what they are and exactly what it will take to fulfill them. Therefore, I strongly encourage you to complete the EMOTIONAL NEEDS ASSESSMENT on the following pages.

Here are some instructions to insure proper outcomes:

1. Review the list of Ten Emotional Needs and ask yourself, *"If I could have ONLY ONE of these needs fulfilled—which one would it be?"* and mark that need with a "1." Next, look at the remaining 9 needs and ask yourself the same question and mark that need with a "2." Continue this process until you have ranked each need in order of priority. Be completely honest with your selections; resist the temptation to manipulate the results.

2. List your top 3 Emotional Needs in the space provided. Just beneath each Emotional Need, list 3 specific ways you would like for your spouse to meet that need. Be as specific as possible.

3. Interview your spouse and note his/her 3 PRIMARY EMOTIONAL NEEDS and the 3 specific ways he/she would like for you to meet them.

Record the information in the space provided.

4. Meet at least one of your mate's PRIMARY EMOTIONAL NEEDS every day and note the outcome: how it made your spouse feel and how it made you feel.

Recommended reading:
His Needs, Her Needs: Building an Affair-Proof Marriage by Willard F. Jr. Harley

EMOTIONAL NEEDS ASSESSMENT

1. Rank your Emotional Needs in order of priority.

   ____ Domestic support   ____ Affection
   ____ Family commitment   ____ Conversation
   ____ Recreational companionship ____ Attractiveness of spouse
   ____ Honesty and openness   ____ Financial support
   ____ Sexual fulfillment   ____ Admiration

2. List your top 3 Emotional Needs in the space below. Just beneath each Emotional Need, list three specific ways you would like for your spouse to meet that need. Be as specific as possible.

Need #1 _____

a. _____

b. _____

c. _____

Need #2 _____

a. _____

b. _____

c. _____

Need #3 _____

a. _____

b. _____

c. _____

3. Interview your spouse and note his/her 3 PRIMARY EMOTIONAL NEEDS and the 3 specific ways he/she would like for you to meet them. Record the information in the space provided.

Need #1 _____

   a. _____

   b. _____

   c. _____

Need #2 _____

   a. _____

   b. _____

   c. _____

Need #3 _____

   a. _____

   b. _____

   c. _____

4. Meet at least one of your mate's PRIMARY EMOTIONAL NEEDS every day and note the outcome:

How did it make your spouse feel?

How did it make you feel?

Chapter Eleven

Fulfilling Emotional Needs

I'm going to start this chapter with a Pop Quiz and I encourage you not to cheat! Resist the temptation to look back at previous chapters and challenge yourself to see how much information you've actually retained thus far.

POP QUIZ

1. List the 9 Fruits of the Spirit in order.

_____ _____ _____

_____ _____ _____

_____ _____ _____

2. Complete the following theory:

The root of anger is a _____ _____.

3. List the Proper Hierarchy of Priorities. (I'll give you the first one.)

    1. God

    2. _____

    3. _____

    4. _____

    5. _____

    6. _____

4. List the Three Levels of Communication (Hint: Iceberg)

    1. _____

    2. _____

    3. _____

5. Write out the L.I.V.E. Communication Technique

    L_____

    I_____

    V_____

    E_____

6. Complete the following statement

When _____ connects with _____, bad things happen!

How well did you do? If you did poorly, it should be an indication that you have not retained many of the important principles and techniques in this book, and you probably need to go back through and re-read the chapters you can't remember. Consider this...

If you don't remember the principles of truth in this book, you cannot apply them. And if you don't apply the truth to your marriage—nothing will change.

Primary Emotional Needs

In chapter ten you learned about 10 Emotional Needs and the importance of those needs being fulfilled—especially your Primary Emotional Needs. By taking the Emotional Needs Assessment, you learned yours and your spouse's 3 Primary Emotional Needs. This chapter will focus on what those Primary Emotional Needs are and what it will take to fulfill them on a long-term basis.

Think about your own and your spouse's top 3 Primary Emotional Needs for a minute. Do you know exactly what to do to fulfill your spouse's Primary Emotional Needs? Does your spouse know exactly what to do to fulfill your Primary Emotional Needs?

If your answer to either of these questions is *No*—you simply MUST go back to the Emotional Needs Assessment and work on it with your spouse until the answer to each of those two questions is a definite *Yes.*

You now have something most other couples do not have: a clear understanding of yours and your spouse's Primary Emotional Needs. The importance of meeting these needs cannot be overstated; it is vital to the health of your marriage.

What did you do this week to fulfill one or more of your mate's Primary Emotional Needs?

Did it feel mechanical or contrived?

Feeling mechanical or contrived is very normal and actually expected when first attempting to meet the newly discovered Emotional Needs of your spouse. You also may have felt a little odd when your spouse attempted to meet one of your needs. You may have even thought, *"Oh, he's only doing this because the book told him to."*

<u>It is very important to understand that the awkwardness will more than likely continue for a season</u>. It's equally important to push through this season of awkwardness until the actions begin to feel normal. Even when the actions feel contrived, you should appreciate your spouse's willingness to try. That, in itself, is very sweet.

Results

Once your needs were met, were you more apt to fulfill your spouse's needs?

It is a fact: you are much more willing to meet your spouse's needs when your needs are met. Therefore, if you want your spouse to fulfill YOUR needs, what can you do to increase the chances of that happening? … That's right: <u>start fulfilling your spouse's needs</u>.

The world (by Satan's influence) has it backwards: they think their needs should be met FIRST, and then, when they are happy, they will be willing to meet the needs of their spouses. <u>It is exactly the opposite</u>. But they have bought into a lie and that's why the divorce rate in our country exceeds 50%.

Now that you can clearly see the benefits of meeting each other's Primary Emotional Needs, your next challenge will be to

REMEMBER WHAT THEY ARE and the specific ways to meet them. One great option is to write your mate's 3 Primary Emotional Needs on a 3" X 5" index card—as well as the specific ways to meet each need. Carry that card with you: wives—put it in your purse; husbands—fold it and put it in your wallet and reference the card every day to insure that you are doing the things needed to fulfill your mate's Primary Emotional Needs.

Hopefully, by now, you have broken The Vicious Argument Cycle. But, for just a moment, go back to that time of arguing, bickering, frustration, stress and contention and answer these questions...

How big was your investment to maintain that mess?
(Probably huge)

How many hours a day?
(Probably several—possibly many)

How many words per day did it take to maintain that mess?
(Probably thousands)

What did it profit your marriage?
(Probably nothing... *zero*)

Now, think of the past few days of fulfilling your spouse's Primary Emotional Needs and answer these questions…

What was your investment to maintain peace and fulfillment?
(Probably very little)

How much time did it take?
(Probably minutes to pay a compliment or help clean up)

How many words did it take?
(Probably just a few; *"Honey, you look really great today!"*)

What did it profit your marriage?
(Probably loads of good feelings and a healthy atmosphere)

Can you see the difference? Your old way took endless hours and words—the atmosphere was tense and burdensome, and there was ZERO PROFIT! But your new way takes just a few words and very little time, but THE PAYOFF IS HUGE!

In the future, you may be tempted to revert back to your old ways of arguing. Hopefully, you will remember this moment and have the Emotional Maturity to use the information you've learned in this book to get your relationship back on track.

The following story will help you remember the importance of meeting your spouse's Primary Emotional Needs.

A woman went to her attorney to start the legal process to divorce her husband. The attorney told her, *"I can have the papers drawn up and delivered to your soon-to-be ex-husband by the end of the week."* The woman replied, *"Oh no; that's much too fast! I want him to hurt as badly as I do, so here's my plan: I'm going to spend the next few months being especially nice to him, make his favorite meals, give him lots of pleasure and cater to his every need—until he is madly in love with me—and then I'm going to divorce him!"*

After three months, the attorney called the woman and asked, *"It's been quite a while since I've heard from you. Are you ready to divorce your husband?"* To which the woman replied, *"Oh no! Things are WONDERFUL now! I've decided to keep him!"*

Moral of the story: fulfill your spouse's Primary Emotional Needs and he/she will be transformed into a spouse you would never want to leave.

Each night this week, sit down with your spouse and discuss the chapters from this book and note how each lesson has affected your marriage.

Write a brief Statement of Commitment to your spouse telling him or her that you are committed to working on your marriage and making it the healthy 'One Flesh' relationship that God intended from the beginning.

Chapter Twelve

Conclusions

For years, I thought couples experiencing marital challenges could simply pray their problems away. As a minister, I would even say things like, *"Only God can heal your marriage."* Even though I sincerely believed that, I began to ask myself, *"Exactly HOW does that happen?"*

I have come to a few conclusions, the first of which is this: a couple experiencing marriage problems is probably not going to walk themselves out of trouble. It is going to take the counsel of an unbiased third party with a biblically-based program to walk them through a process to a healthy marriage.

Another conclusion I've come to is this: we often pray in error. In essence, we ask God to give us a marriage miracle even though we continue to violate His sovereign principles. It simply doesn't work that way; <u>God does not wink at disobedience in order to bless us</u>! He leads us to TRUTH that, when applied, will change our circumstances. And in *that*, we can say, *"God healed our marriage."*

Consider this example: if I were to break out in sores all over my body, I might go to the pharmacist and get a topical cream in hopes of curing the problem. The sores may go away for a few days, but when they come back, I'm going to freak out and rush to see the doctor and say, *"Doctor, look at these sores all over my body!"* The doctor would take a cursory look at the sores, but what is the doctor thinking? He's thinking, *"What bacterium is in Paul's blood that is causing these sores to break out on the surface of his skin?"* He would then draw blood and run some tests and then prescribe an antibiotic (or you could say an *anti-bacterium*) that would correct the ROOT of the problem.

In time, guess what would happen to all the sores? They would slowly go away.

Such is the case with couples that come into our office; they have tried to self-medicate with no success and they are focused on the surface-level problems. They say things like, *"You shouldn't do that to me—it's wrong!"* To which the other will retort, *"Well I only do that because of the way you treat me!"* And the vicious cycle goes round and round. Evie and I, on the other hand, are thinking, *"What is at the root of these problems?"* Once we've identified the *lie* the couple has bought into, we begin to prescribe *truth*. If the couple accepts the truth and applies it to their marriage, guess what happens to their surface-level problems? Yes … they begin to go away.

It is the same with The Marriage Miracle: you must discover the ROOT of the problem—the *lie* that you have inadvertently bought into—and replace it with the anti-lie; the *truth* of God's Word taught in this book. And, by the way, the power of this book is not in any one particular principle or chapter, it is in the sum total of all the lessons. Each builds upon the other.

It really is possible for you to experience a Marriage Miracle but it will not happen with just a wish or a prayer. You've got to do something different. As you apply the truths and principles given in this book you will notice a change in your marriage. It won't happen overnight so don't get discouraged; be patient and consistent and, in time, you will reap the rewards of your investment.

You simply cannot go wrong with truth.

As I stated in the Introduction, this book is part of a twelve-week intensive marriage program called "The Marriage Miracle" that is saving marriages all across the nation. I encourage you and your spouse to consider going through that program. It includes daily homework and a group dynamic that is nothing short of amazing.

Prayer

I'd like to end by praying for you…

Father, You know the needs and challenges the person reading this book is facing. He/she is Your child and I know you care deeply about Your children. You have every answer this reader needs and You will walk beside him/her every step of the way as he/she works to build a solid marriage. I pray that he/she will have the strength and courage to apply Your truth to his/her marriage.

I ask you to give this reader a Marriage Miracle.

In Jesus' name, Amen.

Discover the whole experience at:

TheMarriageMiracle.com

About the Author

Paul Kendall is a minister, author, and host of the nationally syndicated radio program *"Family Matters."* Paul and his wife, Evie, are the Family Pastors at Winston-Salem First and the founders of **The Whole Family, Inc.**, a curriculum company providing programs to churches and corporations that save marriages and strengthen families.

Paul and Evie have been married for 30 years and have two incredible children, Alex and Rene', as well as a wonderful son-in-law, Austin.

Another book by Paul Kendall…

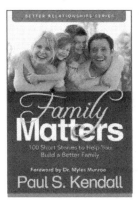

Order online at TheMarriageMiracle.com

Made in the USA
Columbia, SC
04 August 2017